Twelfth Night

AND SHAKESPEARIAN COMEDY

*Three lectures given at the Neptune
Theatre, Halifax, Nova Scotia, as part of
the programme of Dalhousie University
and the Theatre in celebration of the
four hundredth anniversary of
Shakespeare's birth*

TWELFTH
NIGHT
and
Shakespearian
Comedy

Clifford Leech

Dalhousie University Press

University of Toronto Press

© UNIVERSITY OF TORONTO PRESS 1965

Reprinted 1968

Reprinted in 2018
ISBN 978-1-4875-7711-7 (paper)

Printed in the United States of America

PREFACE

The lectures here printed were delivered from the stage of the Neptune Theatre, Halifax, Nova Scotia, in August 1964, as part of a programme arranged by Dalhousie University and the Neptune Theatre to celebrate the four hundredth anniversary of the birth of Shakespeare. This programme also included readings from a number of Shakespeare's comedies, a concert of Elizabethan music, and performances of *Twelfth Night* in the Neptune's summer repertory. The giving of the lectures and their publication were made possible by grants from Dalhousie University and the Canada Council.

What is now published is substantially what was spoken from the stage of the Neptune. A few insertions and changes of wording have been made, and some notes have been added.

I am glad of an opportunity to record my gratitude to my hosts in Halifax, and particularly to Professor S. E. Sprott, who made all the arrangements for the lectures, and Professor A. R. Bevan, the Head of the Department of English at Dalhousie University. I also look back with especial pleasure on the talks I was able to have with Mr. Leon Major, Artistic Director of the Neptune Theatre, and with his talented company of players.

CLIFFORD LEECH

Toronto

CONTENTS

Lecture One

1

THE BEGINNINGS

The story is told that an enthusiastic admirer of Mr. Harold Pinter's play *The Caretaker* went to him one day and said: "Now I have realized what the play is about: it's about God the Father and God the Son." To which the dramatist, we are told, replied: "No. It's about two brothers in a room with a tramp." This response was perhaps as understandably stubborn as Coleridge's on the subject of *The Ancient Mariner*, when he declared that his poem should have been as free from the giving of a moral lesson as the tale from the Arabian Nights which narrated a purely accidental rousing of a genie's desire for revenge.[1] Yet in a sense Mr. Pinter was wholly right. His play takes us to a room owned by two brothers, respectively living there and visiting there. How long that state of affairs has gone on we do not know. But the entire action of the play results from one brother bringing home Davies the tramp: the play concerns itself with the new and developing situation entailed by the temporary existence together of the three characters in one place.

This, indeed, is an ancient form of comedy. The Elizabethans knew it from Terence and Plautus, whose plays have a single locality, in which various characters impinge on one another. The type-action of a Latin comedy is one in which a young man with a clever servant and an unsympathetic father falls in love with a young woman: with the aid of the servant, he finally wins her despite parental opposition. In other words, put certain characters together in a particular place, and work out what happens. It is a good and sufficient formula, whether the place is just any place though happening to have the name of a particular town, or whether it is a rather special place with strong associations or powerful suggestiveness. Shakespeare, adapting the *Menaechmi* of Plautus in his *Comedy of Errors*, changed the locality from Epidamnum, which would mean nothing to Elizabethans, to Ephesus, which they knew well from the Acts of the Apostles as a place where Diana had her temple and unhallowed arts were practised. Mr. Graham Greene in his play *The Living Room* imagined as his locality a room in a large house which had become almost the sole inhabitable room because the two women of the house could not bear to live in a room in which someone had died. Mr. Pinter in *The Caretaker* similarly imagined a room which was a junk-shop of civilization, containing everything from a statue of the Buddha to a non-functioning gas-oven.

The Comedy of Errors is one of the earliest of Shakespeare's plays, perhaps his first comedy, but he frequently used the formula I have indicated. Indeed, basically we find it as late as 1600, in *The Merry Wives of Windsor*. There he takes Falstaff and his companions away from their association with Prince Hal and imagines them impinging on the citizens of Windsor. Falstaff shows his lechery and his belief in his natural gifts: he is brought up against the citizens with their more formidable advantages. And before that, in *Much Ado about Nothing*, Shakespeare showed the complex happenings that resulted when Don Pedro, Don John, Claudio and Benedick came from the wars to the house of Leonato in Messina, where Hero and Beatrice waited for their husbands-to-be. In these plays the locality is always single, the action is the working out of the impingement of characters on one another in that locality. "Bring them together" is the playwright's formula, and the play emerges from interaction.

But there is another formula for comedy, and in this instance there was no classical precedent in the drama. It is a kind of comedy that depends on a change of locality, on the notion of a journey. Its roots lie in Hellenistic romance and more immediately in the sixteenth-century prose narratives that ultimately derive from that. Let a man set out on his travels and let us follow him as he moves from one place to another. Shakespeare used this formula in *The Two Gentlemen of Verona*, where first Valentine and then Proteus leave home and find their way to a ducal court where the Duke's daughter Silvia wins their love. From there they journey farther, to a forest with outlaws, whose king Valentine becomes and who help him ultimately to win the Silvia whose father would have kept her from him. And Julia, the faithful lover of the fickle Proteus, follows her man first to the ducal court and then to the forest. She wins him for a second time, and we hope definitively, after her long journey. This, too, was a mode of comic writing that Shakespeare was to return to. *As You Like It* shows us a shift from Duke Frederick's court to the Forest of Arden, where Rosalind and Orlando can bring their love to fulfilment, and Oliver and Celia, Touchstone and Audrey, can meet. *All's Well that Ends Well* shows Helena at Rousillon, at Paris, in Italy, and again at Rousillon, always in quest of Bertram, whom she falls in love with in Rousillon, traps in Paris and then loses, sleeps with in Italy, and subjugates in Rousillon once more. It is a kind of plot that easily lends itself to the device of disguise: as place is changed, so it is appropriate that personal appearance should be: haven't we often difficulty in recognizing a person out of context?

Yet it will be evident that these two comic modes are not entirely distinct. In the first, a new element is introduced into a hitherto static situation, a single locality. This may be through the accident of a chance meeting of near neighbours: you can suddenly meet for the first time someone who lives almost next door. But more often it comes about through an arrival, the arrival of the tramp in the lives of the two brothers in Mr. Pinter's *The Caretaker*, the arrival in Ephesus of Antipholus of Syracuse, looking for his lost twin, the arrival in Messina of Don Pedro with his officers and his defeated half-brother, the arrival in Illyria of Viola, Sebastian and Antonio. Frequently, indeed, there is the suggestion that a foreign locality, represented by the new arrival, is impinging on the locality that is shown to us. That a new arrival can thus bring with him the sense of a new locality should be particularly evident to us in Canada: his impact on us, and ours on him, will suggest the impact on one another of two localities—as we may feel, too, the impact of province upon province. And this in turn leads to the idea of a play where the essence of the thing is the direct contrast of two localities, both of which are shown to us on the stage. At once we think of *The Merchant of Venice*, with its alternation of Venice and Belmont, of *A Midsummer Night's Dream*, with its alternation of Athens and the wood near-by, of *Twelfth Night*, with its alternation of Orsino's palace and Olivia's house, of *Troilus and Cressida*, with its alternation of Troy and the Greek camp. The comic action in such instances is largely the result of this impingement on one another of two localities, bringing out the special comic character of each.

So we may think of two kinds of comedy—the bringing together and the journeying forth, exemplified especially in two of Shakespeare's earliest plays, *The Comedy of Errors* and *The Two Gentlemen of Verona*—and we may see the fusion of the two kinds in plays where the idea of double locality manifestly underlies, or overtly contributes to, the total structure of the action. But comedy is a complex, or at least various, form of writing, and we must now consider another distinction.

On the one hand, comedy is writing for a festival. It is a sign that, in spite of all, we rejoice at the human situation, we rejoice that difficulties may be overcome and union achieved. The marriages that almost regularly come at the end of comic plays symbolize this idea of union. We have a sense at the close of a comedy that the world is well enough, that we form part of a fellowship, however imperfect. There may be even a "divine comedy," where a devotion to Beatrice is a symbol of a devotion to the cosmos and its ruler and of an ultimate oneness with him. But such a feeling of rejoicing, though strong surely from the birth of European comedy among the Greeks, has a kind of provisional quality. Aren't we, after all, a little too imperfect to achieve a satisfactory union, a satisfactory state of living? Even if we could imagine it for ourselves, can we imagine it for our neighbours? Or perhaps, if our scepticism is of the more modest sort, we may put it the other way round. When this doubt is strong, comedy becomes in large measure the exposure of man's effrontery in thinking he can win his heart's desire. But the doubt may be even more radical, and comedy then becomes an exposure of the triviality of human desire. "Is that all you want?" we may ask of Helena in *All's Well* when Bertram is wedded to her will, or of Olivia and Viola in *Twelfth Night* when they have rather suddenly won their Sebastian and Orsino. In such moments we go back to Aristophanes, the earliest of the major comic dramatists, who, while celebrating the fun he found in human life, simultaneously saw all ambition and pretence as inherently ridiculous. This ultimate comedy thus necessarily combines the sense of triumph with the sense of defeat, a rejoicing in the nature of things with an insistence on human limitations. Lopahin in Chehov's *The Cherry Orchard* wins the estate of Madame Ranevsky, but wins no personal ease or fulfilment. And the same dramatist's Three Sisters experience only a sense of final exclusion when they know that a visit to Moscow is beyond their scope. Even Dante is perhaps not free from this sense of thwarting. He saw the smile of Beatrice and the sempiternal rose in Paradise, but he had to return to the world with only a memory of them. The divine comic mode could offer him a few more years of grief and struggle and an uncertain promise of a fresh long ascent of the purgatorial mountain. No wonder that his mind dwelt strongly on the combativeness of the damned. It will be evident that to combine celebration with critical exposure and with ultimate dubiety requires a most delicate sense of balance: the more inclusive comedy is, the more difficult it becomes to maintain that balance. We shall see something of the difficulty that Shakespeare experienced in *Twelfth Night*.

Tragedy, of course, is another matter. There the writer sees the world as a place where defeat is ultimately total. He may personally entertain a belief in another world in which things are put right, but he is not for the moment concerned with that. What matters for the tragic vision is the defeat, and the ability to face the idea of it. The comic writer, on the other hand, may emphasize either defeat or triumph, but we have seen that he usually insists on the fragility of triumph as well as the triviality of defeat. "Men are as they are, and what of it?" is, in most cases, as far as his comfortable words will stretch. The notion of human grandeur, the catastrophe involving terror and anguish, lie outside his domain. For him, suffering must not be too extreme—if it were, he would not be writing comedy—but it can be poignant, as poignant as it freely is in Chehov or in Ibsen's *The Wild Duck* or in Shakespeare's *Measure for Measure* and *Troilus and Cressida*. Let the sense of terror or anguish intrude, and comedy will be destroyed, for comedy depends on a notion that after all life is livable enough. Even in Stanley Kubrick's film *Dr. Strangelove* we do get to love the Bomb a little. At the heart of comedy there is, in some measure, the sense of acceptance, perhaps too of a desire for betterment but always of a willingness to make merry with things as they are.

But even to make merry we need a means of appraising, a means of demonstrating the comparative goodness of what we may have; and this is the point of the two worlds that are commonly found in Shakespeare's comedies. I have already drawn attention to his frequent use of two localities. Venice can be judged by Belmont, and Belmont by Venice. The Forest of Arden and the court of Duke Frederick have a similarly reciprocal effect: if we value the gentleness of men in the Forest, we can see the comfort and ceremony of the court. Athens and its near-by wood work similarly: we are at home in Athens, even though it is the wood that has finally brought the lovers into the appropriate relationship, and has taught Titania her lesson. So, within a single locality, Shakespearian comedy makes use of two levels of society, which throw light on one another's ideas and which can, as they do in *Love's Labour's Lost*, help to exhibit each other's shortcomings.

As early as *The Two Gentlemen of Verona* this use of social levels becomes a key feature of a play. In *The Comedy of Errors* Shakespeare, improving on Plautus, used two pairs of identical twins, having twin servants in addition to the twin masters he derived from the *Menaechmi*. But in *The Two Gentlemen* the servants operate more powerfully on the way we regard the world of high society. It will be worth devoting a few minutes, I think, to running through the action of this play and seeing in particular how it provides alternation of the high-comic and low-comic characters, and how at certain moments the lower element directly intrudes on the higher. We begin with Valentine and Proteus, the "two gentlemen," devoted to one another but about to be separated because Valentine is to be sent on his travels to complete his education. In Richard Edwards' *Damon and Pithias*, of 1565, the two legendary friends are described as "two gentlemen of Greece" in the list of dramatis personae, and it is apparent that Shakespeare is presenting his audience with two young men who think they share a similar devotion. When Valentine has left, we see Proteus concerned with his love for Julia and employing Valentine's servant Speed in sending a letter to her. The love is made comic through Speed's refusal to look with sufficient seriousness on his mission. Scene ii shows us Julia with her attendant Lucetta: the comedy is continued when Julia pretends to be angry at receiving Proteus' letter and when she tries to put together again the fragments she has torn it into; and Lucetta is ready always to underline her mistress's vulnerability. More soberly, scene iii shows us Proteus in his turn being dispatched on his travels by his father.

Act II takes us to a ducal court where Valentine has fallen in love with the Duke's daughter, and has been reduced to a state where his servant Speed can make unreproved fun of him. It is soon obvious to Speed and to us, but not to Valentine, that Silvia loves him. She has asked him to write a love-letter on her behalf; he has done so, and gives it to her; she thanks him, says "the lines are very quaintly writ" but "I would have had them writ more movingly," and then gives the letter back to him. "Take it for your labour," she says, and leaves him. Valentine needs Speed to explain to him that this has been a confession of love. Then we return to Proteus and Julia, who are saying farewell as Proteus sets out on his travels. Proteus is vocal enough in this short scene, but Julia is almost silent throughout and totally silent after they have kissed. And then in the next scene we first meet Launce, the servant of Proteus. It is odd that Proteus did not use him in Act I when he was sending a letter to Julia, and I think we may assume that he was not in the first plan, or perhaps even first draft, of the play. Certainly he is a different kind of character from Speed. The servant of Valentine belongs with the servant-boys in John Lyly's comedies, but Launce is closer to Lancelot Gobbo in *The Merchant of Venice* and other later figures in Shakespeare who cultivate naïveté even when they appear before us alone. We cannot imagine Speed soliloquizing; we remember Launce best when he has only his dog Crab with him. Launce is to go with Proteus on his travels: he describes the violent lamentations of his father and mother and sister as he took his farewell of them, but he reproaches his dog for its dumb indifference to the proceedings. Proteus, as Julia left him in silence, exclaimed:

> What, gone without a word?
> Ay, so true love should do: it cannot speak;
> For truth hath better deeds than words to grace it.
> [II.ii.16–18][2]

Launce's conclusion is:

Now the dog all this while sheds not a tear, nor speaks a word; but see how I lay the dust with my tears. [II.iii.33–5]

Clearly we are meant to recall the silence of Julia as we hear Launce's reproach. This does not mean that Julia's love is brought into question, but it does prevent us from taking her grief too seriously. Moreover, the vocal Proteus and the vocal Launce and his family are brought into a juxtaposition that makes us ready to doubt the profundity of Proteus' feeling. The parallelism of the two scenes is underlined in that each ends with Panthino, the servant of Proteus' father, entering to urge haste because Proteus and Launce respectively are delaying the journey. We are back with Valentine and Silvia in the next scene, and we find Proteus joining them with a strong recommendation from his friend. But Proteus has only to see Silvia to love her and to want to banish the thought of Julia. It is clear now that the play is going to hinge on a love-friendship conflict, such as John Lyly had made his concern in his famous novel *Euphues* of 1578. After a brief scene in which Speed and Launce talk of their masters' love-affairs and offer a contrast to the high sentence of their masters' cult of friendship, we see Proteus soliloquizing and determining to sacrifice the claims of friendship to those of love. Then, for the last time, we return to the town in which the action began: Julia tells her attendant Lucetta of her decision to follow Proteus in his travels, and to adopt male disguise for the purpose. It is ironic that Julia should set out on Proteus' track immediately after we know he is abandoning her; it is poignant too; and the dramatist does not neglect an opportunity for simple fun in contemplating the notion of a girl in boy's clothes. Lucetta is there to point the irony and the comedy.

This is the end of Act II, and by this time we have seen three characters—Valentine, Proteus and Julia—setting out for the ducal court: their impingement on one another there and in the forest will be the main concern of the rest of the play. The fact that Julia will be in evidence is a kind of guarantee that Proteus will not maintain his inconstancy: Shakespeare throughout his comic career did not underrate the skill of his young women in getting their wishes fulfilled.

But in the first scene of Act III all Valentine's hopes seem dashed. He and Silvia were to have eloped, but Proteus reveals the plan to the Duke, who finds a rope-ladder and a love-letter on Valentine's person and immediately banishes him. He is left to lament his loss of Silvia, and is found in a sad condition by Proteus and Launce. Proteus, of course, pretends a continuing friendship and urges him not to lose hope. But Launce's presence prevents us from taking any of this too seriously. When Proteus and Valentine leave, Launce remains on the stage: he indicates that he already realizes that "my master is a kind of a knave," and then reveals that he too is in love. He is joined by Speed, and tells him in detail of his beloved's characteristics, which he has set down on paper. As he listens to Speed's recital of the list that he himself has prepared, he weighs things up before deciding to pursue his wooing. When, finally, he hears that the girl has "more wealth than faults," he makes up his mind: "Well, I'll have her." The contrast between Valentine's uncalculating devotion and his servant's nice weighing of profit and loss does not put us on Launce's side, but it does make us view the whole matter of love-involvement less seriously. The next scene shows us Proteus pretending to the Duke that he is ready to help on the wooing of the foolish Thurio, the Duke's favourite suitor for his daughter, and there is some wry fun at the expense of love-poetry when Proteus urges Thurio to write sonnets to Silvia and the Duke admits "Ay, / Much is the force of heaven-bred poesy." Perhaps Shakespeare had in mind the words of Mycetes, the foolish

King of Persia in Part I of Marlowe's *Tamburlaine*, who exclaimed: "And 'tis a pretty toy to be a poet." The Duke showed himself to be a comic enough villain when he circuitously revealed Valentine's planned elopement, and his tribute to poetry here is so placed as to bring him to ridicule. Yet not only him: the whole matter of poetry-inflated wooing, the elaborate devising of love-letters, such as Silvia and Valentine had indulged in, is treated with minimal respect.

We are taken to a new locality at the beginning of Act IV. Valentine and Speed find themselves in the hands of outlaws who are looking for a king. If Valentine is willing to take on the office, they are willing to elect him. If not, he must die. Valentine makes his condition:

> I take your offer, and will live with you,
> Provided that you do no outrages
> On silly women or poor passengers.
> [IV.i.70–2]

He is reassured: "No, we detest such vile base practices," although the outlaws have freely confessed to crimes of violence in the past and were ready to put Valentine himself to death. These men of the forest give to the play's last locality an atmosphere of burlesque romance. The next scene shows us Proteus surreptitiously wooing Silvia, watched by the disguised Julia. His wooing includes the singing of the famous song "Who is Silvia? What is she / That all our swains commend her?", and this is given a special irony in that we know the perfidy of the wooer, who is simultaneously being faithless to Valentine, to Thurio (for whom the wooing is being nominally contrived), and to the Julia who, in her disguise, listens and comments. The mocking of love-poetry is thus continued from the previous scene: that the song is a good one makes the irony greater. Then briefly we see Silvia planning to follow Valentine into exile, relying for protection on Eglamour, who has a high reputation in the service of ladies. At this point we meet Launce and his dog Crab once more. The dog has just disgraced himself in public; Launce has claimed that he himself was responsible for this affront to proper standards of behaviour, and has endured the whipping that his dog has earned. Launce's suffering on his dog's behalf makes a comment on Julia's suffering for her devotion to Proteus; and the involvement of servants and masters is made more intricate when we learn that Launce, having been bidden by Proteus to take a fashionable lapdog as a gift to Silvia, had lost it on his way and so had offered his own, quite unfashionable, dog instead. Then we see Julia, who in her male disguise has entered Proteus' service, being sent on a love-embassy to Silvia. Proteus, like Launce, is presenting the wrong ambassador. Julia and Crab once again are bizarrely associated: even the pathos of her situation is given a touch of absurdity.[3]

The first two scenes of Act V show Silvia's escape with Eglamour and its discovery by her father. Then for the rest of the play we are in the forest. The outlaws capture Silvia, who has been quickly abandoned by the knightly Eglamour, but she is taken from them by Proteus, who has followed her. He urges his suit, is repulsed, and then threatens rape. But Valentine has, in some astonishment, witnessed the scene and is, naturally, at this point impelled to intervene. Proteus is stricken with remorse and begs forgiveness. And at once Valentine bestows both forgiveness and Silvia on the erring friend:

> Then I am paid;
> And once again I do receive thee honest.
> Who by repentance is not satisfied
> Is nor of heaven nor earth, for these are pleas'd;
> By penitence th' Eternal's wrath's appeas'd,
> And, that my love may appear plain and free,
> All that was mine in Silvia I give thee.
> [V.iv.77–83]

Julia, who has been present all this while, understandably swoons. When she comes to herself, she is not slow to reveal her identity, and Proteus is shamed into returning to his first love. The outlaws enter with the Duke a captive. Valentine orders his release, and wins his own pardon and acceptance as Silvia's betrothed. Nothing remains but that the outlaws too are pardoned out of hand, and promised employment in the Duke's service.

A great deal of bafflement has been caused by Valentine's willingness to give Silvia to Proteus. Surely, said Sir Arthur Quiller-Couch, at this point we feel there are no gentlemen in Verona.[4] But, urges Dr. Muriel Bradbrook,[5] we must remember the high estimation in which male friendship was held in the sixteenth century. What matters in this play is the friendship: Proteus has betrayed it, but Valentine is true to it. When his erring friend repents, Valentine must show his own truth by giving to that friend exactly what he wishes, in this case Silvia. The young woman is in the background, a mere property to be disposed of when the higher claims of friendship are in question. And certainly it is possible to instance a number of earlier stories in which a young man not merely conquers his own love-feelings but pays no attention to any feelings the girl he loves may have, letting his friend have her simply because he knows that his friend wants her.[6] Nevertheless, I think the historically minded critic of *The Two Gentlemen of Verona* may be in danger of missing the spirit of the play. In going through the action I have wanted to bring out that Shakespeare was continuously making fun of devotion of all kinds. Speed has his brisk mocking mode, and Launce, the shrewd common man enjoying the mask of naïveté that he presents to the world and even to himself when he is alone, brings a robust plain sense to bear on his master and his master's friend and both their loves. Valentine's attachment to Silvia is made a slightly ludicrous thing, as is certainly Proteus' pursuit of her. And so too is Valentine's unswerving belief in his friend's good faith. On the other hand, the resoluteness of both Julia and Silvia, though seen comically, is in sharp contrast to the fragility of the young men's devotion. The strong practicality of Julia's swooning is a triumph of commonsense that Launce would surely approve of. You abandon love to friendship, in fact, only when the love is not too strong. But women have not cultivated friendship to that degree among themselves, or recognized its over-riding claims among men. Valentine's "All that was mine in Silvia I give thee" doesn't have to be taken seriously, however seriously he intends it. The dramatist has been busy enough throughout the play exposing the young men's pretences and their failures to catch up with the growing situation. Valentine had to be told by Speed that Silvia was showing her love when she gave him back the love-letter that he had written for her. Eglamour fled when the outlaws arrived. Proteus, within a single scene, is trans-formed from a would-be ravisher of Silvia to a repentant lover of Julia. Shakespeare is indeed having his fun with all of them, is making us enjoy the spectacle of minor human frailty, and finally celebrates a return to the normal current of life.

He was not the only dramatist of his time to make fun of the friendship cult. We do not know the exact date of either *The Two Gentlemen of Verona* or George Peele's *The Old Wives' Tale*, but we shall not be far wrong in putting them both near the year 1592. Peele's play is a burlesque fairy-tale, in which the hero Eumenides sets out to rescue his love Delia from enchantment. In his quest he meets a friendly ghost, Jack, and he enters into a bargain with him to share equally whatever either of them gains in their adventures. At the end of the play, Delia has been rescued and Eumenides and her two brothers rejoice in their reunion. But then the hero is faced with a problem:

JACK. So, master, now ye think you have done; but I must have a saying to you: you know you and I were partners, I to have half in all you got.

EUM. Why, so thou shalt, Jack.

JACK. Why, then, master, draw your sword, part your lady, let me have half of her presently.

EUM. Why, I hope, Jack, thou dost but jest: I promised thee half I got, but not half my lady.

JACK. But what else, master? have you not gotten her? therefore divide her straight, for I will have half—there is no remedy.

EUM. Well, ere I will falsify my word unto my friend, take her all: here, Jack, I'll give her thee.

JACK. Nay, neither more nor less, master, but even just half.

EUM. Before I will falsify my faith unto my friend, I will divide her: Jack, thou shalt have half.

1ST BRO. Be not so cruel unto our sister, gentle knight.

2ND BRO. O, spare fair Delia! she deserves no death.

EUM. Content yourselves; my word is passed to him.
Therefore prepare thyself, Delia, for thou must die.

DEL. Then farewell, world! adieu, Eumenides!
He offers to strike, and JACK *stays him.*[7]

Jack then assures his friend that his demand was made only in jest and, as a good ghost, he returns unrewarded to the underworld. It is evident that Peele has his fun at the expense of the friendship cult, but in a more overt way than Shakespeare. In *The Old Wives' Tale* the mockery is given a specially broad effect through the obvious echo, in Jack's final intervention, of the Abraham and Isaac story which doubtless some among Peele's spectators had seen played on the stage. Shakespeare's mockery is more indirect, is implied largely through the interaction of the different characters and groups of characters in the play, and has therefore commonly been missed. Nevertheless, if we see the play as working towards a total unified effect (and do not think, for example, of the Launce-scenes as "comic relief"), we shall recognize that Valentine comes within the orbit of our mirth; and this may lead us to look more circumspectly than has always been the case at certain other utterances of figures in the comedies.

So at this point we might consider another and more famous duke.[8] In *A Midsummer Night's Dream*, written perhaps two or three years later than *The Two Gentlemen*, the four wrangling lovers have sorted out their quarrels through their night in the forest, just as Valentine and Proteus and Julia and Silvia managed after all to get things straight when they were in a forest setting, away from the ducal court. Theseus of Athens has been told of the night's adventures and enchantments, but in a famous speech dismisses them as the kind of delusion to which lovers, like poets and lunatics, are necessarily subject:

> I never may believe
> These antique fables, nor these fairy toys.
> Lovers and madmen have such seething brains,
> Such shaping fantasies, that apprehend
> More than cool reason ever comprehends.
> The lunatic, the lover, and the poet,
> Are of imagination all compact.
> One sees more devils than vast hell can hold;
> That is the madman. The lover, all as frantic,
> Sees Helen's beauty in a brow of Egypt.
> The poet's eye, in a fine frenzy rolling,
> Doth glance from heaven to earth, from earth to heaven;
> And as imagination bodies forth
> The forms of things unknown, the poet's pen
> Turns them to shapes, and gives to airy nothing
> A local habitation and a name.
> Such tricks hath strong imagination
> That, if it would but apprehend some joy,

It comprehends some bringer of that joy;
Or in the night, imagining some fear,
How easy is a bush suppos'd a bear?

[V.i.2–22]

Despite the deliberately commonplace ending, the passage as a whole is eloquent and is commonly remembered apart from its context and especially apart from the shrewd comment that follows from Theseus' bride Hippolyta. She notes that there is a consistency in what the four lovers have told, that it is therefore rash to dismiss it all as the working of a love-stricken fancy:

But all the story of the night told over,
And all their minds transfigur'd so together,
More witnesseth than fancy's images,
And grows to something of great constancy,
But howsoever strange and admirable.

[V.i.23–7]

And we know, because we have watched the comedy, that they haven't deceived themselves, that some force external to themselves has brought matters into harmony. In *A Midsummer Night's Dream* that force has been presented in the shape of the fairies and their king Oberon. He and they stand for the spirit of comedy, that kind of comedy that celebrates both the subordination of men to a Way of the World that they cannot understand and a free acceptance of, and delight in, that subordination. It is arrogant of Theseus to explain things away, and this comedy of the *Dream* ends appropriately at night-time once more, with the fairies entering the Duke's palace, blessing the now married lovers, and then directly addressing us who have watched the spectacle. And, of course, in this play Shakespeare has made fun of the drama too, as Bottom and his fellows act their "very tragical mirth" of Pyramus and Thisbe. "The best in this kind are but shadows," says Theseus, and we may decide that the best of dukes too is but a shadow of what he thinks himself to be. For all his dignity, Theseus has something of Bottom's self-confidence.

The comedy of Shakespeare's early years is essentially the comedy of festival, but it is informed also by a spirit of scepticism. The festival involves an unmasking, a recognition of pretence and error—though the characters themselves, as in the *Dream*, may not realize what has happened. Sometimes the unmasking is accompanied by a reunion of those who have been separated, as when the two sets of twin brothers find each other in *The Comedy of Errors*, and the separated parents of the Antipholuses emerge respectively from the convent and from the shadow of judicial death. Or as when Proteus recognizes the disguised Julia who has followed him. Or as when Demetrius, aided by the fairy's charm, looks with love upon the Helena he had abandoned. In *Love's Labour's Lost* the King of Navarre and his followers come to recognize the unpracticality, for them, of a life of seclusion and study. At the end of each play it is the normal world whose force is reasserted, a world that had gone in some measure awry, either through accident, as in *The Comedy of Errors*, or through a lover's passing fancy, as in *The Two Gentlemen of Verona* and *A Midsummer Night's Dream*, or through an over-ambitious desire to move above the normal level, as in *Love's Labour's Lost*. So the everyday current of life is celebrated, with, however, the dramatist's sufficient recognition that, though acceptable enough, it is lacking in any special glory. The young men of these comedies are prone to error and pretence: if they suffer a shock, it does not make them any the less puny. Valentine's most notorious act in *The Two Gentlemen of Verona* was to offer Silvia to Proteus; his last act in the play was to recommend his unruly outlaws to the Duke's service. If the one action shows an imperfection in his love, the other has at least an equal rashness. Certainly the young women of these plays come off rather better. The Princess of France and her ladies are the skilled instructors of their lovers; Julia shows resolution in following Proteus, and an adequate knowledge of the right moment to swoon. But neither Julia nor Silvia, neither Hermia nor Helena in *A Midsummer Night's Dream*, and not the Fairy Queen herself, is proof against absurdity. If on the whole the women depart less from commonsense than the men, they share a general if engaging fragility.

At the beginning of this lecture I referred to the singleness of place which was characteristic of classical comedy and which Shakespeare used in *The Comedy of Errors* and *Love's Labour's Lost* and returned to some years later in *The Merry Wives of Windsor*. However, it appears that he came to see the advantage of a change of locality, and the idea of a journey is strong not only in *The Two Gentlemen of Verona* but in *A Midsummer Night's Dream* as well as in the later comedies we shall be concerned with next. As already noticed, even when the action is confined to a single locality the idea of a journey has some part in the economy of the play. Aegeon and Antipholus and Dromio have come from Syracuse to Ephesus and thus made possible the encounters that take place in the scene of the action. The Princess of France and her ladies have journeyed from her father's court to Navarre, and it is their arrival that precipitates the end of pretence in the kingdom that is directly presented to us. Shakespeare in these years seems to be working towards the direct impingement of place upon place, as he was to show it in a series of plays including *The Merchant of Venice, As You Like It* and *The Winter's Tale*. To some extent it is a contrasting of the country and the town (a contrasting implicit in the whole pastoral tradition), with a suggestion of a greater modesty of ambition, a smaller degree of pretence in the country. But it is not always as simple as that, as we see in *Love's Labour's Lost*. And where an actual journey is part of the play's action, as in *The Two Gentlemen of Verona*, the tangles are straightened partly because the characters are removed from the place where the tangles have come into being. It is, after all, a common enough matter of experience that we see things differently when we make a change of place: a state of mind is bound up in some measure with the locality in which it was generated. Not that Shakespeare suggests we always feel differently when we make a move. Julia does, oddly enough, love Proteus everywhere, as Orlando and Rosalind were to love in the Forest of Arden though they had fallen in love in Duke Frederick's court. But in that Forest Oliver was to lose his hatred for Orlando and become an acceptable husband for Celia, and Duke Frederick himself had only to arrive at the fringe of the Forest to feel ripe for conversion by a conveniently encountered hermit. Part of the cheerful scepticism of these plays resides in man's vulnerability both to a change of place and to the impact of a visitation from outside. Antipholus of Ephesus lived in a fairly untroubled fashion, despite the shrewishness of his wife, until the visitors from Syracuse came. The course of study proposed by the King of Navarre is brought to an abrupt end through a visitation from Paris. Proteus was led to near-disaster through being sent away to complete his education. Demetrius entered the Athenian wood in pursuit of Hermia, and emerged from it in love with Helena. These things represent a mode of experience that Shakespeare was to explore again in the comedies that followed.

The later comedies, however, have a strain in them that we have not noticed here. I have emphasized in discussing

The Two Gentlemen of Verona that we are always pre-
vented from being much disturbed by the threats of disaster
and the moments of sorrow. Launce and Speed are ready
to belittle their masters' concerns; the Duke is too small a
person to make us feel he will get any part of his way;
Proteus at his most villainous is not clever enough to look
dangerous. If Aegeon is sentenced to death in the first
scene of *The Comedy of Errors,* we quickly learn that his
lost sons are near and we are in no doubt that he will escape
execution at the day's end. Only in *Love's Labour's Lost* is
there a true and cold touch of a sharper reality. A messenger appears from the court of France and announces the
King's death. This is sobering, and brings the King of
Navarre and his lords to a straightforward declaration of
their loves. But it is no moment for an immediate making
of matches. The women put the men on trial: they must
renew their suit in a year's time, and Rosaline is especially
precise in dictating terms to Berowne:

> You shall this twelvemonth term from day to day
> Visit the speechless sick, and still converse
> With groaning wretches; and your task shall be,
> With all the fierce endeavour of your wit,
> To enforce the pained impotent to smile.
> [V.ii.860–4]

He recognizes the task for what it is, and admits his
incapacity:

> To move wild laughter in the throat of death?
> It cannot be; it is impossible;
> Mirth cannot move a soul in agony.
> [V.ii.865–7]

But Rosaline indicates that he will learn from this the
limits of his power over others. The play comes to its end
with songs of spring and winter, emphasizing the cycle of
the year and the ever-repeated disappointment of spring's

promise, the ever-repeated termination of festival-time. The very last words of the play are of separation: "You that way: we this way." Perhaps *Love's Labour's Lost* as we have it is a revised text, but certainly we can say that, alone among the early comedies, it has a disturbing quality that we shall meet later: a recognition of unappeasable suffering, of death and recurrent destruction, of an imperfection that is not easily faced. As this strain grows in his comic writing, it makes Shakespeare's hold on the idea of comedy a precarious one. In the plays that lie ahead, including *Twelfth Night*, we are sometimes not sure whether the picture of the world is any longer truly, or at least wholly, comic.

NOTES TO LECTURE 1

1. Coleridge, *Table Talk* for 31 May 1830.
2. Quotations from Shakespeare are from *The Complete Works*, ed. Peter Alexander (London, 1951). Act, scene and line references are from the Globe edition.
3. On this and other examples of comic juxtaposition in the play, see Harold F. Brooks, "Two Clowns in a Comedy (to say nothing of the Dog): Speed, Launce (and Crab) in 'The Two Gentlemen of Verona,'" *Essays and Studies 1963*, pp. 91–100.
4. *The Two Gentlemen of Verona* ("New Cambridge" edition, 1921, reprinted 1955), p. xiv.
5. *Shakespeare and Elizabethan Poetry* (1951), pp. 147 ff.
6. MacEdward Leach in his edition of the medieval romance *Amis and Amiloun* (Early English Text Society, 1937) noted eighty-six examples of this type of story. One that seems to have been in Shakespeare's mind in writing his play is the story of Titus and Gisippus, told by Sir Thomas Elyot in *The Governor* (1531) as well as elsewhere.
7. Text from *Five Elizabethan Comedies*, ed. A. K. McIlwraith (World's Classics, 1934).
8. I have commented on the general comic fallibility of Shakespeare's dukes in "Shakespeare's Comic Dukes," *Review of English Literature*, V (April 1964), 101–14.

Lecture Two

2

TWELFTH NIGHT,
OR WHAT DELIGHTS YOU

In 1910 Shaw wrote a brief play called *The Dark Lady of the Sonnets* in which he showed us Shakespeare urging Queen Elizabeth to establish a National Theatre in England. It has taken a long time for that to come about, but at least it has happened now, in time for Shakespeare's quatercentenary. In talking to the Queen, Shaw's Shakespeare argues that the public won't support the kind of play he wishes to write, so he has got into the habit of giving them what they demand. Here are the words that the later dramatist puts into the mouth of his predecessor:

Only when there is a matter of a murder, or a plot, or a pretty youth in petticoats, or some naughty tale of wantonness, will your subjects pay the great cost of good players and their finery, with a little profit to boot. To prove this I will tell you that I have written two noble and excellent plays setting forth the advancement of women of high nature and fruitful industry even as your Majesty is: the one a skilful physician, the other a sister devoted to good works. I have also stole from a book of idle wanton tales two of the most damnable foolishnesses in the world, in the one of which a woman goeth in man's attire and maketh impudent love to her swain, who pleaseth the groundlings by overthrowing a wrestler; whilst, in the other, one of the same kidney sheweth her wit by saying endless naughtinesses to a gentleman as lewd as herself. I have writ these to save my friends from penury, yet shewing my scorn for such follies and for them that praise them by calling the one As Y o u Like It, meaning that it is not as *I* like it, and the other Much Ado About Nothing, as it truly is. And now these two filthy pieces drive their nobler fellows from the stage, where indeed I cannot have my lady physician presented at all, she being too honest a woman for the taste of the town.[1]

In this dismissal of *Much Ado* and *As You Like It* as being not at all to the taste of an ambitious dramatist, Shaw is silent about *Twelfth Night, or What You Will*—whether because he thought it better, or because it would not fit so neatly into his sentence as the other plays did, we can hardly know. But there can be no question that in this group of three comedies, almost certainly Shakespeare's most popular comic plays and generally regarded as his best in that kind, he was developing the practices that we noted in my first lecture. The idea of a journey in *As You Like It*, the coming of strangers in *Twelfth Night*, the return to Messina of the victorious Don Pedro and his defeated half-brother Don John in *Much Ado*—these things precipitate the main actions of the three plays. We have, moreover, the impingement on one another of two social worlds, notably in the way the thick-witted Dogberry and Verges bring to light the truth about Hero, a truth which the people of high society are incapable of establishing, and in the interaction of the different social strata in Olivia's household. In general the mockery in these plays is gentle, and at the same time there are touches of a harsher aspect of things such as we have seen in the ending of *Love's Labour's Lost*. Nevertheless, there is not much harshness here, and Shaw would appear right in seeing these plays as predominantly ministering to an audience's pleasure. He was doubtless wrong in assuming—if indeed he did assume it—that Shakespeare despised that pleasure, for one can hardly manage to write an *As You Like It* unless one happens to enjoy what one is doing. Even so, they are plays of exclusion: the dramatist, as well as the spectator, knows well enough that this presentation of life is not the whole truth. He is satisfied to see for a moment some of the more pleasing aspects of human experience, aspects that may be only occasionally available and never enduring, but discoverable none the less from time to time.

They are not plays—and this is particularly true of *As You Like It* and *Twelfth Night*—with a great deal of laughter in them. Rather, they seem to give the finest embodiment in English of the kind of comedy that Sir Philip Sidney talked of in his *Apology for Poetry*, written about 1580, before Shakespeare began to write and when secular English drama had hardly advanced beyond infancy. Sidney saw comedy as twofold, dependent either on laughter or on "delight," though he did not deny that the two could be found together in the same play. Urging that "the whole tract of a comedy should be full of delight," he went on:

But our comedians think there is no delight without laughter; which is very wrong, for though laughter may come with delight, yet cometh it not of delight, as though delight should be the cause of laughter; but well may one thing breed both together. Nay, rather in themselves they have, as it were, a kind of contrariety: for delight we scarcely do but in things that have a conveniency to ourselves or to the general nature: laughter almost ever cometh of things most disproportioned to ourselves and nature. Delight hath a joy in it, either permanent or present. Laughter hath only a scornful tickling. For example, we are ravished with delight to see a fair woman, and yet are far from being moved to laughter. We laugh at deformed creatures, wherein certainly we cannot delight. . . . Yet deny I not but that they may go well together. For as in Alexander's picture well set out we delight without laughter, and in twenty mad antics we laugh without delight, so in Hercules, painted with his great beard and furious countenance, in woman's attire, spinning at Omphale's commandment, it breedeth both delight and laughter. For the representing of so strange a power in love procureth delight: and the scornfulness of the action stirreth laughter.[2]

We rejoice or delight in the gracefulness of the spectacle that *As You Like It* or *Twelfth Night* offers us: the characters may fall into absurdity, and then we shall laugh, but in general we are with them, admiring, almost, the way they live up to their own natures and exert themselves on the stage without impeding the total movement towards harmony in the close.

And yet, as I have already suggested, the idea of such a comedy brings with it a necessary doubt. The more expertly the dramatist writes, the more difficult it is to prevent our mental reservations from getting in the way of a full response to the comedy. And the more profound the dramatist's understanding, the more likely he is to introduce covert qualifications of his own. Of the three plays of this kind that Shakespeare wrote around the year 1600, the last was, by common agreement, *Twelfth Night*: it is the least robust, the most fragile, and consequently the play that most of all seems to hint at the dramatist's own dubiety. It can be performed broadly or prettily or sadly. Sir Tyrone Guthrie has made it into almost a "dark comedy." To bring out its full character is not easy, and in the rest of this lecture I want to concentrate attention on this play. It will be evident that, in an attempt to analyse, I shall be trying to suggest both the sense of "delight" that the play gives and the sense of the extreme vulnerability of that delight. Compared with *Twelfth Night*, the plays I spoke of in my first lecture are secure celebrations, where the exclusion of much of human life is easily and confidently achieved. The rarification of Shakespearian comedy in his play of Illyria is necessarily accompanied by a realization that the extreme term has been reached, that in the very moment of purest "delight" the attitude of acceptance has become almost impossible to maintain.

First of all I should like to glance at the play's stage-history. Dr. Leslie Hotson has argued that it was written for performance on 6 January 1601 at Whitehall Palace,[3] but that is a matter of conjecture to which we must return. We know of later performances at the Middle Temple on 2 February 1602, and at court on 6 April 1618 and 2 February 1623:[4] on the last of these occasions the play is called "Malvolio" in the court records, an interesting early hint of where the chief centre of attention lies for some spectators. In the early Restoration years it was seen three times by Samuel Pepys, who found it "a silly play," "one of the weakest plays that ever I saw on the stage."[5] But we do not know of any performance of *Twelfth Night* after 1669 until the curious version of William Burnaby was acted in 1703 with the title *Love Betray'd; or, The Agreable Disappointment.*[6]

Burnaby's re-writing is little read now, but it is worth examination as an attempt to bring Shakespeare's comedy into relation with early eighteenth-century taste. Its scene was not an imagined Illyria but a commonplace sort of Venice, a place of rapidly developed affection and farcical intrigue. Olivia, here called Villaretta, is a gay and cynical young widow whose passion for the disguised Cesario is not taken very seriously. Malvolio and Sir Andrew are combined in one character, a comic butler who is made to believe that his mistress loves him. Shakespeare's elaborate gulling of Malvolio is reduced to a simple conversation

in which the butler is told of his mistress's love and begins
to preen himself on his imminent elevation. One sees at
once that *Love Betray'd* is written for a smaller stage than
Twelfth Night, and in a theatrical manner in which speed
is everything. Shakespeare's scene, where we watch
Malvolio finding and reading the letter, with Sir Toby, Sir
Andrew and Fabian eavesdropping on him and freely
making their comments on his behaviour, demands a large
stage and a leisurely tempo. Burnaby in the early eighteenth
century eschewed the prolonged soliloquy and relied on a
brisk interchange between two or three characters. Yet
Love Betray'd is not without its complications: it begins
in rakish prose, close to the usual manner of comedies
written for the Restoration stage, with Villaretta (or Olivia)
scornful of the married state; as it proceeds, more and more
of the dialogue is in blank verse (some of it, indeed, Shakespeare's) and the tone shifts towards the sentimental. It
ends in the moralizing strain characteristic of sentimental
comedy, as Moreno (or Orsino) declares:

> Now the Adventures of the Day are over;
> We may look back with pleasure on our Toils,
> And thro' the various turns this truth observe;
> That Honesty is still the care of Providence!

By *Rodoregue,* we see that good will wait upon a worthy
action—By *Sebastian,* that Fortune can't long stain an honest
Friendship.

> *And here I find, that some kind Star above,*
> *Has still a Blessing left for Honest Love.*[7]

But this change of manner and feeling in *Love Betray'd* is
a superficial one. There is nothing disturbing in the play.
It is simply that Burnaby has moved from one theatrical
mode to another, whereas in Shakespeare there is a continuous tension. The core of *Twelfth Night* is given to
us in the first act: Orsino's and Olivia's affectation of sad-

ness, Viola's mingling of staunchness and love and acquiescence, and the variegated world of Oliva's household (including the shrewdly impertinent Feste, the indrawn Malvolio, the robustly contemptuous Sir Toby, the busy Maria)—all these are elements consistently present, and prominent, in the play to its end. It is only when we look through them and discern that none of them is presented without a touch of mistrust, that we experience difficulty in seeing the play as an at once graspable whole. Burnaby's confusions in his version of the story are the result of casual and indifferent craftsmanship; Shakespeare's complexities arise from the nature of his experience as a human being. Certainly if we give ourselves the exercise of reading *Love Betray'd*, we shall think the more respectfully of *Twelfth Night*. One is made aware, too, of how the three-dimensional Shakespearian stage fitted the Shakespearian complexity, enabling the dramatist to juxtapose contrasted characters, like Malvolio on the one hand and his eavesdroppers on the other, and to weld together soliloquy and *sotto voce* comment, while the shallower stage of the early eighteenth century, where the actors stood out sharply from their painted background, invited the simpler clashes of a flat theatrical world.

The modern history of *Twelfth Night* dates from 1741, when Macklin played Malvolio.[8] That performance is the first that we know of after *Love Betray'd* made its last appearance in 1705. The fact that Macklin chose the part of Malvolio is an indication that, as in 1623, the steward seemed an important element in the play's composition. During the following two centuries the play has never been long absent from the London stage. But the actors have not always been content to play the text as it appears in the First Folio. John Philip Kemble's acting edition, published in 1810, makes a number of changes, including the transposition of the first and second scenes. In recent years directors have frequently followed Kemble in thus giving the dialogue between Viola and the Captain before taking us to the lovesick Illyrian court. The reason for the change is fairly obvious. We begin, as it were, outside the play's setting, as in *The Tempest* we begin on a ship off the coast of the enchanted island, and thus are brought more gradually to the play's heart. This method of slow approach is to be found both in Elizabethan and in more modern drama. Apart from *The Tempest*, we have it in Ben Jonson's *Bartholomew Fair*, where the opening scene introduces us to the Littlewit household and to the other characters on their way to the Fair: our notion of Bartholomew-pleasures is sharpened by the postponement of arrival. So, too, it is only after the first act of *Othello* that we reach Cyprus, where Iago's plots are to take shape and Othello's long agony is to run its course. And in Ibsen's *The Wild Duck* we do not reach the Ekdals' dwelling-place until after we have spent the tail-end of an elegant evening with Old Werle. Indeed at first glance it would appear that Kemble's alteration to *Twelfth Night* is an obvious improvement, and the only explanation of why Shakespeare did not arrange things in Kemble's way is, I think, that he did not see Viola's function in the comedy as so important as directors and critics have made it in the last hundred and fifty years. If we begin with Viola, we are likely to see her as the bringer of sanity and truth to an Illyria sick with affectation. But it is not Viola but the accidents of the plot that make Olivia and Orsino come to terms with life, and she has nothing to do with the gulling of Malvolio or his growth in stature. At the end it is Feste, not Viola, who brings us away from Illyria to the place and time we live in. Viola, in fact, is not a disruptive element, a reformer of the Illyrian emotional condition: she is an honorary

Illyrian from the moment of her appearance. So, attractive in many ways as it appears, modern directors seem in error when they follow Kemble in making this alteration.

On various occasions, however, other freedoms have been permitted. In 1820 the dramatist Frederic Reynolds helped to diversify the comedy by the introduction of "Songs, Glees, and Choruses, the Poetry selected *entirely* from the Plays, Poems, and Sonnets of Shakespeare."[9] In more recent years the words of the text have generally been thought sufficient, but a performance at Stratford-upon-Avon in 1947 showed us Orsino's courtiers exercising themselves with Indian clubs while their Duke tried their patience with his talk of music as the food of love, and in the Hebrew version of the play acted by the Habimah company, the National Theatre of Israel, Malvolio is a corpulent buffoon who is made ultimately to see the joke against himself and is persuaded to join Sir Toby and Sir Andrew in throwing paper-darts among the audience.[10] Both these details of production were remote from Shakespeare's intention, but one sees the motives behind them. Unless we look carefully at the play's beginning, we do I think find Orsino's lines merely cloying, and the director who brought in the Indian clubs was manifesting his own reaction to the scene. And Malvolio is a problem, as Charles Lamb saw in his essay "On Some of the Old Actors": however easily we may talk about the appropriateness of his discomfiture, his final appearance induces a wry and uncomfortable laughter, and we are not quite to be entreated to a peace. Nevertheless, the play shrinks if we smooth away its roughnesses. We do it no service if, like Burnaby in *Love Betray'd*, we flatten it out. I think the Indian clubs were wrong, because we need to listen to Orsino's words and to take them seriously: they say more, perhaps, than we readily remember. I think the Habimah company was wrong in its treatment of Malvolio, because the most interesting thing in *Twelfth Night* is its ultimate drawing back from a secure sense of harmony. Yet these persistent attempts to refashion parts of the play suggest that, for all its popularity, it has made each generation feel, to some small extent, ill at ease. This should be remembered when we consider some of the play's obscurer elements.

Fairly recently two well-known scholars have each devoted a volume to this comedy: Professor John W. Draper with *The Twelfth Night of Shakespeare's Audience*[11] and Dr. Leslie Hotson with *The First Night of Twelfth Night*. Very different pictures of the play are given in these books, yet they both depart from the usual notion of it. Neither is in tune with Sir Arthur Quiller-Couch's idea of *Twelfth Night* as Shakespeare's last pure comedy, with its gaiety poignant and the more precious in that the end of peace is in sight.[12] For these robuster scholars, Illyria is no world of the fancy, to be entered only through theatrical magic. For Professor Draper, Illyria is everyday London, with its hazards, its insecurities, its makeshift solutions. For Dr. Hotson, it is a mirror of Whitehall Palace, presenting to the courtly gazers cunningly twisted reflections of their own selves. For both of them the play is good journeyman's work—Dr. Hotson astonishingly believes that only ten or eleven days elapsed between the commissioning of the play and its first performance—and there is no room in either interpretation for dissonance or ambiguity. For Professor Draper, it appears, *Twelfth Night* is not very far away from the most realistic of Jonson's comedies. He calls it "Shakespeare's play of social security," for he finds in it several characters who are trying to secure or to preserve for themselves a comfortable niche in the social structure. Feste goes to Orsino's court, not because

Shakespeare wanted a singer there or thought it good to link Orsino's and Olivia's households through the presence of Feste in both places, but because the Fool wants to establish good relations with the Duke who seems likely to marry the Fool's mistress; the dowerless Maria schemes to marry a gentleman; Sir Toby is anxious to keep Olivia's roof over his head; Sir Andrew is a usurer's son who looks to a noble marriage; Malvolio is dangerously ambitious. Even if we could accept Professor Draper's conjectures about the origins and the motives of the characters, we should feel one major lack in his interpretation: he seems to leave no room for laughter and none for "delight." We ought apparently to feel only relief when Olivia is proof against Sir Andrew's wooing, or when Malvolio is reduced to a simple object of contempt. However, we are apparently to accept Maria's marriage with Sir Toby, and Olivia's continued toleration of her undisciplined uncle, because these things will not seriously disturb the Elizabethan hierarchies.

One gets the impression that Professor Draper has not recently seen the play on the stage. In the theatre, in whatever style it is produced, it does make a rather different impression from a leading article in *The Economist*. It is as well to remind ourselves that in the early seventeenth century this comedy was found comic, and especially so by virtue of its characterization of Malvolio. Leonard Digges, writing commendatory verses for the edition of Shakespeare's poems published in 1640, contrasted Ben Jonson's loss of popular favour with Shakespeare's continued success. Digges's memory of the plays was perhaps imperfect, for he appears to put Beatrice and Benedick in the same play as Malvolio, but this confusion brings out all the more clearly what feature of *Twelfth Night* had remained fast in his mind. He says:

let but *Beatrice*
And *Benedicke* be seene, loe in a trice
The Cockpit Galleries, Boxes, all are full
To hear *Maluoglio* that crosse garter'd Gull.[13]

Evidently Digges at least did not see the play as primarily a social comment.

Dr. Hotson, however, finds plenty of food for laughter. For him the play is a Twelfth Night revel, given at Whitehall in leap year. Because it is leap year, the women do the wooing; because the place of performance is Elizabeth's court, there are continual references in the play to public figures and to the court precincts. The occasion of first performance was 6 January 1600 Old Style, when Elizabeth was entertaining Don Virginio Orsino, Duke of Bracciano, and when Russian ambassadors were also in London. Olivia is a graceful image of the Queen; Orsino is a courtly homager of hers, a maker of fitting compliments, not a man rather comically lovesick. Malvolio, on the other hand, is a disrespectful portrayal, licensed by the Lord Chamberlain, of Sir William Knollys, Controller of the Queen's Household. Dr. Hotson believes, too, that Shakespeare makes fun of the Russian embassy when Viola, acting as Orsino's messenger to Olivia, finds herself put out of her part, as the Russians themselves had recently been. No one would deny the possibility of topical reference in an Elizabethan comedy, but Dr. Hotson's reconstruction of the first performance of *Twelfth Night* is open to suspicion on at least two counts. First, as Sir Walter Greg pointed out in letters published in *The Times Literary Supplement*, 6 January 1600 Old Style was not in leap year: February 29 came in the year 1599–1600, not 1600–1601.[14] Secondly, the normal practice in professional performances at court was for the actors to give a play in which they were already well versed through performances in the public theatre. This is apart from the near-impossibility of our crediting the idea that *Twelfth Night* was composed and rehearsed in ten or eleven days, as is required by Dr. Hotson's reconstruction of the circumstances of its first performance. Certainly Shakespeare's use of the name Orsino may echo the real Orsino's visit to Elizabeth, but one wonders if the Duke, had he been present at a performance of the play, would have welcomed his presentation as so melancholy and yet so changeable a wooer, and the exchange of his real dukedom of Bracciano for that of Illyria, a country notorious, Dr. Hotson reminds us, for riot and piracy. Certainly Malvolio and the ridiculous costume he is persuaded to wear may be a hit at some man of the court, noted for his self-importance and for an unfitly amorous temper, but we can hardly share Dr. Hotson's certainty in establishing the identification. With all such efforts to find real-life originals for dramatic characters and situations, one needs to keep a measure of scepticism. Moreover, even if some of our identifications are correct, they contribute only a small part of the comedy's statement. A play lives through its presentation of the general properties of human nature, which are given individuality within the dramatic composition. The use of contemporary caricature, though it may often be useful to the dramatist as a starting point for his characterization and his comic incident, can of its very nature have only a transient interest. *Twelfth Night* has long been popular with audiences who have known nothing of the topicalities of Elizabeth's court. Even at Stratford-upon-Avon, when we see Malvolio smiling and cross-gartered, we do not, in a scholarly way, turn to our neighbour and remark: "Master Controller, to the life!" What Shakespeare did with Malvolio and Orsino was to demonstrate the more amusing side of self-love and of love for woman. We have owed much to Dr. Hotson over the years for his diligent uncovering of forgotten event, but this book, even if his conjectures approached the convincing, would hardly skim the surface of the play. If Professor Draper is too solemn in his account of the matter, Dr. Hotson's laughter is altogether too ready. He is anxious not to miss a single joke, and we may feel that he misses almost everything else.

The speculations of these scholars are not likely, in the long run, to prevail against the traditional view of the play. That view, as far as it goes, is surely in accord with our own responses. The play is gay and a little sad and certainly high-fantastical. Its material is human nature, but the angle of vision is unusual, the range of vision highly selective. And for the fun and ingenuity of it we are invited, and are willing, to take a little of the impossible as a seasoning to genuine observation. Illyria is not everyday Elizabethan London or even the court at Whitehall. It is a land with some of its own laws, where things ripen fast, and sometimes with grace, where men are almost always at leisure for love or wine or practical jesting. Its humour, as we have noted, is less sharp than is often found in comedy: if at the end Malvolio is at odds with his fellows, they at least feel a warm desire that rancour should not be nourished.[15] Were the play all this and nothing more, it would give us much to take pleasure in. But there remains that sense of uneasy affection that the play does, I think, generally induce. To see *Twelfth Night* is to be reminded of occasions when we are making merry with those who are closest to us in sympathy and affection, and yet, though the pleasure is keen and genuine, we are fractionally conscious that the formula is not quite right, so that we cannot quite keep it from ourselves that an effort is needed for the contrivance of harmony. On such occasions the moment comes when we look coldly on the merry-making and the good relationship and see the precariousness of our tolerance for one another, the degree of pretence in all sociability. But that moment of disillusioned insight does not invalidate the experience of brief rejoicing that is possible in human encounters. There is an important sense in which any goodness in life is an artifact. Illyria, with the events it frames, is Shakespeare's image for this contrived thing: it impresses us the more deeply because from time to time Shakespeare seems deliberately to make us aware of the contrivance. The ways in which he does this will be my concern in the remainder of this lecture.

And first, of course, there is the problem of Malvolio. Lamb says: "I confess that I never saw the catastrophe of this character, while Bensley played it, without a kind of tragic interest."[16] But in saying that, Lamb has rather bedevilled the issue. We are not concerned with tragedy in *Twelfth Night*. "Tragedy" implies a whole view of the universe, in which man's sureness of defeat is seen at odds with his magnitude of spirit. The dominant attitude of *Twelfth Night* is far from that: the play is concerned, rather, with man's subjection to a relatively kindly puppet-master, and Malvolio, however he may suffer, is not a symbol of human greatness. If we are to look for a resemblance between him and other Shakespearian characters, we shall find his kin not among the tragic heroes but rather in the Parolles of *All's Well that Ends Well*. Parolles is a braggart and a coward, who is finally exposed when he shows himself willing to buy his life with treachery. The world of *All's Well* is much darker than that of *Twelfth Night*, and fittingly, therefore, Parolles' failings are deeper than Malvolio's. But their resemblance lies in our response to their humiliation. Both of them become aware of solitude. When that happens to Parolles, he shows an interesting resilience: "Even the thing I am shall make me live," he says, and he is willing to accept the scorn of men who are safe in their noble station, if they will, nevertheless, find a place in their charity for him. Malvolio shows not resilience but a sense of outrage. "Madam, you have done me wrong, notorious wrong" is his cry to Olivia when he is brought from the darkness of his cell to the bright end of the comedy, and his final words, "I'll be revenged on the whole pack of you," leave us uneasy at the gull's intransigence and wincing at the word "pack." Thus he becomes a stronger, more independent figure than Parolles, but they are alike in our sense of discomfort in their baiting. Illyria, like the France and Italy of *All's Well*, cannot exist without a strain of cruelty, of persecution. We cannot have our Illyria, in fact, without an echo of the common world. Even Sir Toby, who has been a prime mover in the gulling of Malvolio, confesses he is uneasy about what has been done:

I would we were well rid of this knavery. If he may be conveniently delivered, I would he were, for I am now so far in offence with my niece, that I cannot pursue with any safety this sport to the upshot. [IV.ii.72–7]

And Olivia and the Duke, the persons of authority in this play's world, are anxious that all shall be put right. Yet it is apparent that it cannot be put right. The humiliation of Malvolio is the price that one pays for practical jesting: one cannot strip the self-important and the puritanical without sharing their embarrassment at nakedness. To put Malvolio on a tragic level is to disregard the general effect of his appearance on the stage: rather, he is one of those comic figures at whom it is too easy to laugh, so easy that, before we know it, we have done harm and are ashamed. At the end of *All's Well* we may feel more in sympathy with Parolles than with any other character. That is not the case with Malvolio and *Twelfth Night*, for the dominant mood of this comedy is gentler and we are here more closely in tune with the dénouement.

Yet even in this relaxed comedy, with its conclusion in Viola's victory over Orsino's heart and Olivia's winning at least the appearance of the man she had fallen in love with, we are not long allowed to forget the harshness of things. Malvolio is suddenly brought to Olivia's mind in the last scene because Viola mentions the imprisonment "at Malvolio's suit" of the captain who had helped her when she arrived in Illyria. It is evident that the ambitious steward has exercised authority with a long arm: our realization of that moderates our pity for him. Then, when "the madly us'd Malvolio" is brought onstage, and the whole story is told, Feste runs through the matter of the gulling, with a special sourness in recalling how Malvolio had spoken contemptuously of him at the beginning of the play. Audiences in the Neptune Theatre will I think be conscious of the sharp and emphatic way in which this production's Feste, Mr. David Renton, delivered these lines:

Why, "Some are born great, some achieve greatness, and some have greatness thrown upon them." I was one, sir, in this interlude—one Sir Topas, sir; but that's all one. "By the Lord, fool, I am not mad!" But do you remember—"Madam, why laugh you at such a barren rascal? An you smile not, he's gagg'd"? And thus the whirligig of time brings in his revenges.
[V.i.378–85]

It is hard to be reminded of one's own words, especially at the moment of humiliation, and Feste's remorselessness here, while not putting us on Malvolio's side, makes us realize what it is like to be in his situation. The "whirligig of time" only for a moment appears to be a light-hearted and irreverent way of referring to Fortune's wheel: the fun evaporates with the word "revenges." This is a vindictive Fortune, a Fortune who not only turns her wheel but punishes. Her spokesman is the clever and engaging Fool.

Against Fortune, against the general laughter of Orsino's and Olivia's people, there stands the mock-madman madly used, the petty tyrant who now in his turn talks of revenge. We are made conscious that this despised man, the man outside the orbit of harmony, makes, almost like Gregers Werle in Ibsen's *The Wild Duck*, his "demand of the ideal." We feel, like Olivia and the Duke, the pity of life's refusal even in this comedy to sort itself out with a uniformity of happiness. The play is the stronger for its sense of this impossibility.

There are other traces of human suffering in this play. Antonio's relation with Sebastian has its poignancy. On his first appearance he tells Sebastian of the danger he runs in coming near Orsino's court, but he is willing to risk that to be near his friend. His language here is curiously emphatic:

> I have many enemies in Orsino's court,
> Else would I very shortly see thee there.
> But come what may, I do adore thee so
> That danger shall seem sport, and I will go.
> [II.i.46–9]

"Adore" is a strong word in Shakespeare. It prepares us for Antonio's violence of language when he believes that Sebastian has betrayed him in his time of necessity:

> ANT. Let me speak a little. This youth that you see here
> I snatch'd one half out of the jaws of death,
> Reliev'd him with such sanctity of love,
> And to his image, which methought did promise
> Most venerable worth, did I devotion.
> 1 OFF. What's that to us? The time goes by; away.
> ANT. But, O, how vile an idol proves this god!
> Thou hast, Sebastian, done good feature shame.
> In nature there's no blemish but the mind:
> None can be call'd deform'd but the unkind.
> Virtue is beauty; but the beauteous evil
> Are empty trunks, o'erflourish'd by the devil.
> 1 OFF. The man grows mad. Away with him.
> [III.iv.393–405]

And in the last scene of the comedy he speaks at length of his "love" and of the ingratitude it has met with:

> A witchcraft drew me hither:
> That most ingrateful boy there by your side
> From the rude sea's enrag'd and foamy mouth
> Did I redeem; a wreck past hope he was.
> His life I gave him, and did thereto add
> My love without retention or restraint,
> All his in dedication; for his sake,
> Did I expose myself, pure for his love,
> Into the danger of this adverse town;
> Drew to defend him when he was beset;
> Where being apprehended, his false cunning,
> Not meaning to partake with me in danger,
> Taught him to face me out of his acquaintance,
> And grew a twenty years removed thing
> While one could wink.
>
> [V.i.79–93]

Immediately afterwards Orsino is reproaching the disguised Viola in similar terms, thinking that the boy he has befriended has shown a perfidy like that which Antonio has believed himself to find in Sebastian: the parallelism is comic and prevents us from taking Antonio's plight overseriously for more than a moment. Yet for that moment he brings to us a strong sense of disillusioned friendship. If we compare it with Valentine's disappointment with Proteus in *The Two Gentlemen of Verona*, we see that here Shakespeare has much more fully imagined the situation. And while Antonio remains on the stage, we have before us a reminder that humanity is vulnerable through its attachments, that affection puts a man in another's power.

Now we have a more difficult matter to turn to. On the Elizabethan stage the women's parts were of course played by boys, and some time before Shakespeare began to write the dramatists saw the piquancy of a situation in which a boy-player, acting the part of a young woman, had to wear the dramatic disguise of a boy. This could produce sexual overtones of a complicated kind, and the effect was increased rather than diminished by the general reticence in Elizabethan times concerning homosexual feeling. References to such feelings are rare and usually brief in the drama, though Marlowe, as we might expect, becomes explicit on the subject in *Edward II* and, in relation to the god Jupiter, in *Dido Queen of Carthage*. Apart from the strong weight of religious and social condemnation, the use of boy-players for the women's parts would make overt homosexual reference a hazardous matter for the theatre. But in a number of Elizabethan plays, and *Twelfth Night* is among them, the sexual situation may at moments appear tangled.

One of the earliest sixteenth-century plays in which a girl-character is disguised as a boy is John Lyly's *Gallathea*, probably first acted shortly before 1588.[17] In that play the scene is Lincolnshire, and we are told that every year Neptune sends a monster to devour "the fairest and chastest virgin in all the countrey." Two shepherds, each convinced that his daughter qualifies for election, separately decide that a male disguise is the best means of escape. So the girls Gallathea and Phillida are made to wear boys' clothes: they meet and fall in love. In the end Venus brings them help: Gallathea and Phillida shall proceed to church for a marriage ceremony, and the goddess undertakes that one of them shall change her sex at the church door. The fact that the play was performed by the Children of Paul's at their private theatre and at court would simultaneously make the action possible on an Elizabethan stage and increase its effect of over-ripe fantasy. We have evidence enough that Shakespeare was familiar with Lyly's writings, and in *Twelfth Night* there is a palpable reminiscence of *Gallathea*.[18] When Gallathea and Phillida are beginning to suspect that they are of the same sex, this exchange takes place:

PHIL. Haue you euer a Sister?
GALLA. If I had but one, my brother must needs haue two; but
I pray haue you euer a one?
PHIL. My Father had but one daughter, and therefore I could
haue no sister.

[III.ii.36–40]

In *Twelfth Night* we find Viola telling the Duke of her imaginary sister's unhappy love, and then this question and answer:

DUKE. But died thy sister of her love, my boy?
VIO. I am all the daughters of my father's house,
And all the brothers too—

[II.iv.122–4]

Shakespeare's way of writing is a long way from Lyly's repetitive prose, but we can hardly avoid the impression that *Gallathea* was somewhere in his mind as he led Viola through her masquerade. He is not prurient here, as Lyly appears to be, but the scenes in which Olivia falls in love with, and makes overtures to, a seeming boy do not leave us without embarrassment. More than usually in Shakespeare we are made conscious of the sex of the players, the sex of the characters they are playing, and the double disguise of the boy playing Viola. The thing is a jest, but we cannot take it quite light-heartedly because of the extent to which Shakespeare has suggested a disturbance of mind in both Olivia and Viola. We are not in the world of the Christmas pantomime of the English theatre, with its principal-girl and principal-boy, both played by actresses, where the affections are only conventionally suggested: Olivia, conscious of her love for a mere page, as she thinks, has a touch of Angelo's shame in *Measure for Measure*, when he finds the saintly Isabella arousing his lust; and Viola, more aware of the situation, can exclaim in soliloquy:

> Disguise, I see thou art a wickedness
> Wherein the pregnant enemy does much.
> [II.ii.28–9]

The tone of her speech as a whole remains comparatively light, but the vocabulary is weighted in these two lines. We may contrast the incident in *As You Like It* where Phebe falls in love with the disguised Rosalind: that is never suggestive of deep feeling in Phebe's case or of anything but amusement in Rosalind's.

It is difficult to speak of this element in *Twelfth Night* without appearing to exaggerate its significance in the whole pattern, and we must remember that in a modern production the use of actresses for the women's parts materially lessens the disturbing quality. Because on our stage the transvestism is single and not double, the effect has not the specially troubling character that emerges when a boy playing a girl becomes emotionally involved with a boy playing a girl disguised as a boy: with that complexity we reach a point where sexual distinctions begin to dissolve. If we can imagine the play as acted at Shakespeare's Globe Theatre, we may feel that Illyrian love is presented with a touch of wryness, that a jovial absurdity is not its only hazard.

Moreover, the ending of the play suggests a refusal to take a love-attachment with a full measure of sympathy. Orsino turns quickly from Olivia to Viola, as years before Proteus in *The Two Gentlemen of Verona* had turned from Silvia to Julia. And Olivia is content with Viola's brother, having married him in place of the boy-girl-boy that had banished her own brother's memory. So much, it seems implied, for rhapsody of all sorts.

As comic error may arouse a sense of danger, so the lyric

fluency of *Twelfth Night*'s verse may sometimes disguise
a quality of harshness in what is said and may, on the other
hand, sometimes provoke a resistance in the hearer through
an over-cultivation of the dying fall. In the play's opening
Orsino is languorous at love's and music's joint command:

> If music be the food of love, play on,
> Give me excess of it, that, surfeiting,
> The appetite may sicken and so die.
> That strain again! It had a dying fall;
> O, it came o'er my ear like the sweet sound
> That breathes upon a bank of violets,
> Stealing and giving odour!
>
> [I.i.1–7]

Two lines later the Duke turns his thought to love's power
to destroy: nothing, he says, will keep its worth in the love-
charged mind, which has room for but one value:

> O spirit of love, how quick and fresh art thou!
> That, notwithstanding thy capacity
> Receiveth as the sea, nought enters there,
> Of what validity and pitch soe'er,
> But falls into abatement and low price
> Even in a minute.
>
> [I.i.9–14]

We may think of the lovesick Troilus and Paris in *Troilus
and Cressida*, for whom the laws of Nature and of nations,
the continuance of their city's life, were no things of
moment, and we may remember that *Troilus and Cressida*
was probably written within a year or two of *Twelfth
Night*. Almost immediately afterwards Orsino speaks of
love's disregard even for the lover: when first he saw
Olivia, he tells us,

> That instant was I turn'd into a hart,
> And my desires, like fell and cruel hounds,
> E'er since pursue me.
>
> [I.i.21–3]

This is extravagant talk, of course, the small change of

Elizabethan sonneteers, uttered by a man who finds a measure of enjoyment in the suffering he describes. Even so, the violence of the image (muted as it is by its familiarity and its implied classical reference to Actaeon) is in counterpoint with the verbal fluency.

The most famous love-passages in the play, those where devotion is most freely and picturesquely embodied, have a cloyingness that comes near to dulling our appetite and to making us question the impulse behind them. That the effect was operative for Shakespeare as it is for us is, I think, evident from the frankness of Orsino's words (whatever their tone). And when Olivia's beauty is unveiled in I.v, there is a startling bluntness in Viola's comment: "Excellently done, if God did all." The remark embarrasses Dr. Hotson, for he is convinced that Olivia's character is a courtly image of Queen Elizabeth, and it is well known how strenuously the ageing Queen depended on cosmetic aid.[19] But there is no need to bring Elizabeth in here. The line has a sharpness in its general reference, in its scepticism and note of challenge, in its envy and impatience of the power of beauty. As we have seen, Sidney saw comedy as depending on the spectator's "delight," on his acceptance of the controlled and often absurd motions of the characters for the sake of the graceful pattern that is made. But the kind of comedy that holds us most conveys a hint of resentment too. Madame Ranevsky in *The Cherry Orchard*, Alceste in *Le Misanthrope*, Volpone in Jonson's play, the lovers in *The Way of the World*—all these must utter the words and perform the actions that their characters and situations decree, and there is a pleasing appropriateness in their varying discomfitures; yet along with our pleasure goes a greater or less, a never wholly subdued, never dominant, regret that things are as they are. *Twelfth Night* has hardly the inclusiveness of the comedies that I have just mentioned. Yet it shares their sense of recoil; from it, too, from what it implies but cannot of its nature put over-plainly, we infer the limitations of the comic form.

At the very end of the play, the dramatist gives over the comic idea. Feste sings his epilogue, bringing us back from Illyria to the wind and the rain that every day beat on human heads. It is not uncommon to suggest that at the end of a comedy we emerge from a dream to a waking condition. In the Prologue at Court to Lyly's *Sapho and Phao* Elizabeth is asked to grant the players the licence of a dream-world:

in all humblenesse we all, & I on knee for all, entreate, that your Highnesse imagine your self to be in a deepe dreame, that staying the conclusion, in your rising your Majestie vouchsafe but to saye, *And so you awakte.* [Prologue at the Court, 14–17]

Puck at the end of *A Midsummer Night's Dream* has a similar plea:

> If we shadows have offended,
> Think but this, and all is mended,
> That you have but slumb'red here
> While these visions did appear.
> And this weak and idle theme,
> No more yielding but a dream,
> Gentles, do not reprehend.
> [V.i.430–6]

But Feste's conclusion to *Twelfth Night* is more than the use of a tried formula. We owe to Dr. Hotson a useful analysis of this song, in which his wealth of understanding of Elizabethan English is put to good account. He seems, however, to miss altogether the poignancy of its grossness. He shows us that the Fool's "foolish thing" is both his professional bauble and a phallus, and the song runs through a rake's progress of lechery and drunkenness and rejection by society.[20] But this epilogue to *Twelfth Night*

has an epilogue of its own in the heart of *King Lear*. There
we find an additional stanza for the song:

> He that has and a little tiny wit
> With heigh-ho, the wind and the rain—
> Must make content with his fortunes fit,
> Though the rain it raineth every day.
> [III.ii.74–7]

It is again a Fool singing, and the "tiny wit" is in implied
antithesis to the great bauble and the other thing that he
carries. Now the stress is on human vulnerability and the
human desire to come to terms. In *Twelfth Night* there
was something of truculence in Feste's ending. Men's gates
have been shut against him, his swaggering has not availed
him, his cups have brought headache and ignoble company,
and this has been making a continuous pattern since "A
great while ago the world begun"; yet he confesses it all
with a shrug and a defiance, and ends by reminding us that
he is an entertainer. He has amused us, and enriched our
transient Illyria, but will not let us go without claiming
a common humanity with us. He is a player as well as an
imaginary character: we can meet him outside the theatre
when the performance is over, and the life-conditions that
we know belong to him too. He has a descendant in the
Archie Rice of John Osborne's *The Entertainer*, who ended
that play by asking us to let him know where we were
working tomorrow: he was ready to exchange rôles and to
come and watch us.

The shifting of viewpoint that comes with the *Twelfth
Night* epilogue is remarkable. Orsino has, in the last lines
of the play itself, referred to Viola as "Orsino's mistress and
his fancy's queen," and for the moment we seem securely
in the world of make-believe, the world where the clue to
love's labyrinth is successfully followed, where fancy is
free and yet has its queen. And then at once we are among

toss-pots and their drunken heads. Yet the transition is bridged by music. Feste has been a singer, of love and of "good life," within the play, and it is therefore in character that his epilogue should be sung. In the 1800 Preface to the *Lyrical Ballads* Wordsworth pointed out that the use of metrical form could soften the effect of a painful narrative.[21] Even more powerful in this respect is the singing voice. Shakespeare here dismisses his comedy and our acceptance of it, but the total effect is not harsh. We leave the theatre with a tune in our ears, and the harmony of *Twelfth Night* is after a fashion maintained. Later we may recall what Feste's words have been, as we recall Malvolio's treatment and the other disturbing reverberations of the comedy, but none of them will, during the time of performance or the time it takes to leave the theatre, obtrude much on our consciousness. There has, after all, been song at Illyria's departure from us.

NOTES TO LECTURE II

1. *The Works of Bernard Shaw* (London, 1930), XIII, 248.
2. *English Critical Essays (Sixteenth, Seventeenth, and Eighteenth Centuries)*, ed. Edmund D. Jones (World's Classics, 1922), pp. 56–7.
3. Leslie Hotson, *The First Night of Twelfth Night* (London, 1954), pp. 13 ff.
4. E. K. Chambers, *William Shakespeare: A Study of Facts and Problems* (Oxford, 1930), II, 327–8, 346.
5. *The Diary of Samuel Pepys*, ed. H. B. Wheatley (London, 1904–5), III, 6; VIII, 193.
6. Allardyce Nicoll, *A History of English Drama 1660–1900*, II (Cambridge, 1952), 301.
7. Text from *The Dramatic Works of William Burnaby*, ed. F. E. Budd (London, 1931).
8. Charles Beecher Hogan, *Shakespeare in the Theatre 1701–1800*, I (Oxford, 1952), 455.
9. *Twelfth Night* ("New Cambridge" edition, 1930, reprinted 1959), pp. 176–7.
10. The Habimah production of *Twelfth Night* was given eighty-seven times, being acted for the first time in Berlin on 15 September 1930 and for the last time in Israel on 9 April 1946. The director was Mikhail Chikhov. (Information kindly provided by the Habimah Theatre, Tel-Aviv, and by Professor D. A. Fineman.)

I was able to see the production at the Phoenix Theatre, London, soon after the first performance.

11. John W. Draper, *The Twelfth Night of Shakespeare's Audience* (Stanford and London, 1950).

12. *Twelfth Night* ("New Cambridge" edition), pp. xxvii–xxviii.

13. Chambers, *William Shakespeare*, II, 233.

14. *The Times Literary Supplement*, 31 December 1954, p. 853; 28 January 1955, p. 57.

15. Feste should be excepted: see p. 45.

16. *Essays of Elia* (World's Classics, 1901, reprinted 1903), p. 189.

17. The anonymous *Sir Clyamon and Sir Clamydes* (c. 1570) is the earliest known English play to use the device.

18. Cf. *The Complete Works of John Lyly*, ed. R. Warwick Bond (Oxford, 1902), II, 569. Quotations from Lyly are from this edition.

19. Hotson, *First Night*, p. 132.

20. *Ibid.*, pp. 167–72.

21. Wordsworth, *Poetical Works*, ed. E. de Selincourt, II (Oxford, 1944), 399–400.

Lecture Three

3

COHERENCE REGAINED

Shakespearian comedy after *Twelfth Night* is of a different order, or rather of several different orders. There is the farce of *The Merry Wives of Windsor*, there are the "dark comedies" or, as they are sometimes called, "problem comedies" (*Troilus and Cressida, All's Well that Ends Well* and *Measure for Measure*), and there is the group of romances that come at the end of his career as an independent dramatist. This is indeed a varied collection, and the term "comedy" may seem stretched when we apply it to all these plays. The editors of the 1623 Shakespeare Folio saw *Troilus and Cressida* and the romance *Cymbeline* as tragedies, and there are many scholars and critics today who agree with them over *Troilus*.[1] Nevertheless, I am going to discuss this contentious play and *The Winter's Tale*, which seems to me the most ambitious and most comprehensive play in the romance-group, and to present them as constituting Shakespeare's supreme work in forms of comedy where the notion of "delight" is no longer dominant. Different as they are from one another, they share a total quality of "coherence," a quality that *Twelfth Night* and the other major comedies of around 1600 did not fully achieve. In my last lecture I tried to suggest that, because it aims so fully at "delight," *Twelfth Night* is especially fragile and capable of interpretation and performance in a wide variety of ways. We are never quite sure what the dramatist is doing, never quite sure of the degree of stress he wishes a particular element in the play to bear. But in *Troilus and Cressida* and *The Winter's Tale* he was, I think, in full mastery of his aim. For all the complexity that characterizes both, there can be no doubt of the way we are to see these plays. It is true that academic interpretations have been varied with both of them, but I do not think that in performance there is a great variety of effect. Here the theatre seems an altogether more reliable guide than what emerges from the study.

They are widely separate in date. *Troilus and Cressida* was probably written in 1601 or 1602, perhaps a year after *Hamlet*, two years after *Twelfth Night*. *The Winter's Tale* came some nine years later, just after *Cymbeline*, just before *The Tempest*. In between lie three of the four great tragedies and the Roman plays *Antony and Cleopatra* and *Coriolanus*. And not merely in relation to their dates of composition these two pieces of writing are as far apart as two writings can be while coming from the same man in the years of his maturity.

Troilus and Cressida is nearer in manner and spirit to the comedies of Ben Jonson than any other play that Shakespeare wrote. In 1602 Jonson had not yet written his finest work: *Volpone* was to come in 1606, and *The Alchemist* and *Bartholomew Fair* some years after that. But from 1599 he had been experimenting with a kind of comedy that was admittedly influenced by Aristophanes, a kind of comedy which depended on exposing to the audience's laughter a series of character-types. He called his plays of this kind "comicall satyres," and the term underlines the fact that we are here far from the comedy of "delight." We are meant to recognize deformity, grossness, overweening and destructive pretence. Shakespeare may have written *Troilus and Cressida* for performance at one of the London Inns of Court, where the audience would be homogeneous, sophisticated, highly literate. In any event, we have evidence that it was not performed at the Globe Theatre. It looks, moreover, as if Shakespeare deliberately set out here to write in some measure after Jonson's example. In showing us the beef-witted Ajax, the emulous and cruel and passionate Achilles, the *voyeur* Pandarus, the railer Thersites, the frail Cressida, the deluded Troilus, he offers a gallery of character-types that invite our judgment. Yet we shall see that his play is more complex than the "comicall satyres" of Jonson, that it embodies a more profoundly experienced and considered vision of human life, that there is, in addition, a degree of human sympathy in it that Jonson at that time rigorously eschewed.

Shakespeare also parts company with Jonson in his choice of theme and setting. Although one of the "comicall satyres" —*The Poetaster* of 1601—does take us to the court of Augustus in Rome, Jonson does not employ for any of his comedies a major series of events from world history or legend. Shakespeare, on the other hand, takes us to Troy and shows the turning-point in the war for Helen. This at once gives a suggestion of weight and seriousness.

The story of the siege was not merely a European legend of great antiquity. The epics of Homer and much Greek drama derive from it; Vergil chose for the hero of his Roman epic a fugitive from the stricken city, and retold in the early part of *The Aeneid* the story of Troy's destruction. And Troy was strongly remembered all through the Middle Ages. England, indeed, came to have a special relationship with the story. The legend grew up that

Brutus, a grandson of Aeneas, colonized the island and that the name "Britain" was derived from him. London was thus a Trojan city, and it was frequently called "New Troy." This legend was still in existence in Shakespeare's time, though perhaps the belief in it was growing a little polite. Even as late as 1612, the dramatist Thomas Dekker called his Lord Mayor's Pageant for that year *Troia-Noua Triumphans*. In such a context, it was inevitable that English sympathies should be strongly on the side of the Trojans, and this would be increased by the pro-Trojan sympathies of Vergil, the poet of antiquity for whom most men of the time felt a special veneration. Consequently, a writer who chose the siege as a subject for a play would be expected to show partiality on the Trojan side.

Yet at once in *Troilus and Cressida* Shakespeare makes it plain that he has no such simple partiality. There is a prologue to the play, which begins with a deliberately rhetorical description of the Greek forces making their way to Troy, and suddenly this falls into anticlimax with the mention of the reason why the expedition has been undertaken:

> their vow is made
> To ransack Troy, within whose strong immures
> The ravish'd Helen, Menelaus' queen,
> With wanton Paris sleeps—and that's the quarrel.
> [Prologue, 7–10]

No more slighting, though no more restrained, indication of a cause of war could be imagined. The prologue goes on to describe the Greek landing and the Trojan preparation for defence, and there follows a contemptuous comment on the feeling generated on both sides:

> Now expectation, tickling skittish spirits
> On one and other side, Troyan and Greek,
> Sets all on hazard.
> [Prologue, 20–2]

We may think back two years, to the time when Shakespeare wrote *Henry V* and described the enthusiasm of
young Englishmen for the King's campaign against France:

> Now all the youth of England are on fire,
> And silken dalliance in the wardrobe lies;
> Now thrive the armourers, and honour's thought
> Reigns solely in the breast of every man.
> [II, Prologue, 1-4]

Henry V was not free from some satiric thrusts at the kind
of thing that leads to war, the kind of thing that happens
in war, but the contrast between the lines quoted from the
two plays illustrates a considerable change of emphasis.
Now the two sides in the war are not differentiated; the
spirits of those excited at the thought of fighting are
"tickled," "skittish." Men wholly worthy of respect, the
prologue suggests to us, would not wager their own and
others' lives for such a trifle as the identity of Helen's bed-
fellow. And the prologue concludes with an invitation to
the audience to like or dislike the play as they wish: their
decision, however, on whether it is good or bad will be as
much a matter of chance as the winning or losing of a war.
In other words, not only is this particular war fought for
a trifling cause: to settle any matter by war is no more a
guarantee of justice than the drawing of lots, though rather
more costly. We are again a long way from *Henry V*, with
its king's declaration that the triumph at Agincourt is God's;
but of course Shakespeare in *Troilus* was in a freer position
than in the earlier play: patriotic feeling was not so profoundly involved, and he was writing in a pre-Christian
framework which allowed him to indicate a divine imparti-
ality.

The neutrality and measured venom of the prologue are
echoed during the play. "Fools on both sides" is how Troilus
apostrophizes Greeks and Trojans in the first scene, and the

Greek Diomed later becomes sourly eloquent when Paris protests that he has spoken bitterly about his countrywoman Helen:

> She's bitter to her country. Hear me, Paris:
> For every false drop in her bawdy veins
> A Grecian's life hath sunk; for every scruple
> Of her contaminated carrion weight
> A Troyan hath been slain; since she could speak,
> She hath not given so many good words breath
> As for her Greeks and Troyans suff'red death.
> [IV. i. 68–74]

There is no doubt that Shakespeare's play strongly implies the absurdity of fighting for Helen, and sees folly and suffering on both sides in the war.

Yet Shakespeare does suggest a difference between Greeks and Trojans. Each suffers from a particular delusion. For the Trojans the delusion is "honour," the idea that there is necessarily glory in fighting and dying for the cause of one's choice. But Hector, the chief man of Troy, the most esteemed of King Priam's sons, knows that one first needs to be sure of the goodness of one's cause. He knows, too, that a decision on the place where Helen sleeps is not a matter of moment, and he argues eloquently that both the law of Nature and the law of "each well-order'd nation" demand that she shall be returned to her husband, the Greek Menelaus. Troilus, his brother, suggests that the very idea of "value" is arbitrary, that the value of a thing is what man has imposed on it, that Greeks and Trojans have chosen to put a high value on Helen, who has thus become a proper cause of war. And, even more interestingly, he argues that in committing oneself to a cause one has given a permanent commitment, as in the taking of a wife. But Hector insists on the inherency of value, denying that man can decide for himself what is and is not valuable: the hard implication of this argument is that one is bound to the duty of continuous re-assessment. Yet suddenly, at the end of the council scene in Troy where this exchange takes place, Hector goes against his own better judgment and agrees with the views of Paris and Troilus—his "sprightly brethren," he calls them—that they must continue the war and fight for Helen.

The Trojans, indeed, strive to believe that the war is a courtly game. This pretence can mask from them the dread face of permanent commitment. If they are "sprightly," if they dress the war up in chivalric disguise, both its hard reality and the destruction that confronts Troy can be put from their thoughts. Hector challenges the Greeks to produce a champion who will fight with him to decide whose wife is more virtuous and more beautiful. Not surprisingly, the Greeks are a little perplexed, though feeling a need to live up to the courtly fashion their opponents have set before them.

For the Greeks the delusion is more subtle and insidious. They think that a man is, or can be, governed by reason. Achilles, their chief fighter, is sulking in his tent, unwilling to return to battle. In the council of the Greeks, Ulysses argues that the withdrawal of Achilles is subverting the notion of "degree," that every man in the army is now ready to disregard his duty because Achilles is so obviously neglectful of the authority of the Greek leader Agamemnon. Ulysses, in his famous speech on "degree," presents a picture of the universe in which everything in the skies and on the earth, every man in his society, must conform to the order of behaviour which is appropriate to him. Any departure from this will lead to chaos.[2] But Achilles, the man most concerned, is not present when Ulysses argues in this way. Having convinced Agamemnon and the rest that Achilles must be brought back to the war, Ulysses plots with Nestor—the aged man who, ironically, represents the accumulated

Greek wisdom—to conduct a fake lottery in order to decide which Greek shall meet Hector's challenge: they will see to it that Ajax, not Achilles, is chosen, and this will make Achilles feel that his supremacy among the Greeks is no longer certain. Then Ulysses goes to Achilles and talks to him about "emulation." This is the impulse that he had condemned when speaking to the other Greek leaders, to whom he declared that each man should keep to his place. To Achilles he urges:

> Keep then the path,
> For emulation hath a thousand sons
> That one by one pursue; if you give way,
> Or hedge aside from the direct forthright,
> Like to an enter'd tide they all rush by
> And leave you hindmost;
> Or, like a gallant horse fall'n in first rank,
> Lie there for pavement to the abject rear,
> O'er-run and trampled on. Then what they do in present,
> Though less than yours in past, must o'ertop yours;
> For Time is like a fashionable host,
> That slightly shakes his parting guest by th' hand;
> And with his arms out-stretch'd, as he would fly,
> Grasps in the comer. The welcome ever smiles,
> And farewell goes out sighing. O, let not virtue seek
> Remuneration for the thing it was;
> For beauty, wit,
> High birth, vigour of bone, desert in service,
> Love, friendship, charity, are subjects all
> To envious and calumniating Time.
>
> [III.iii.155–74]

This, he says, is the

> One touch of nature [that] makes the whole world kin—
> That all with one consent praise new-born gawds,
> Though they are made and moulded of things past,
> And give to dust that is a little gilt
> More laud than gilt o'erdusted.
>
> [III.iii.175–9]

Thus for Achilles he presents the world as a chaos in which each man must strive to do better than his neighbour or be crushed by him; to the other Greek leaders he argues that each man must observe his place in the interest of the whole. Ulysses nearly succeeds, however, in persuading Achilles, through his politic reasoning, to return to the war. But only nearly, because Achilles then gets a letter from Troy: he is in love with Polyxena, and her mother Hecuba, Queen of Troy, asks him not to return to the fighting. That overrides Ulysses' argument: for his love's sake, Achilles will forget the call of reason. Nevertheless, in the end he does take up arms again. His "male varlet" Patroclus is killed by Hector. Ulysses' arguments were defeated by the claims of love; those claims in their turn cannot withstand the desire for revenge. He returns to the field to kill Hector, because Hector has killed his friend. In retrospect we see that Ulysses' pretended appeal to reason (in his talk with Achilles) was an appeal to self-interest, to a passion for reputation. It was less strong than love, which in its turn was less strong then the desire for revenge. Men do not come near acting for the sake of the abstract "value" (which even Hector finally spurned for the sake of "honour") or for the sake of preserving the hierarchies of "degree." Whether or not the publicly argued concepts of Hector (value) and Ulysses (degree) are right, they have no effect on what men do. And it is the baser passion (revenge) that is the most operative.

The killing of Hector is brutal. The two men meet in the battle, but Achilles, getting the worse of it, is ready to flee. Hector, as so often with his mind on "honour," willingly allows this. Then Hector is attracted by the sight of a nonentity in splendid armour, and kills him for it. He thinks the day's fighting is done, and puts by his own arms. Achilles and his followers find him: unarmed, one against many, he is butchered. Ironically, this immediately follows his abandonment of the pursuit of "honour" for the pursuit of a particularly fine sort of battle-dress. Again the baser passion has taken precedence.

So far I have spoken of the story of the war, the story of Achilles and Hector and Ulysses. But this play is called *Troilus and Cressida*. The prologue makes no mention of the lovers: that silence makes up for the exclusive stress on them in the play's title. We meet Troilus in the first scene, where he describes Cressida as a "pearl" which he must make a long voyage to possess. He is impatient, yet childishly dependent on the good offices of Pandarus, Cressida's uncle. At this point we can hardly take the love affair seriously. Is Cressida worth so much ado, any more than Helen is worth the fighting of a war? Then Shakespeare presents her on the stage as a young woman with shrewdness and a mocking tongue. She makes fun of her uncle the pander; she admits in soliloquy that she has long loved Troilus; and there is no doubt that she has a keen sense of the world about her. She is, in fact, a good deal more alive and interesting than the arch and passée Helen who appears in one brief scene of the play. When Cressida and Troilus actually meet, she suddenly speaks with a new and moving directness. He has been speculating on whether he will be able to preserve a sense of "distinction in his joys," and in their first exchanges they have fenced with one another in discreetly bawdy prose. But then Cressida changes the medium to blank verse and makes a simple avowal:

> Boldness comes to me now and brings me heart.
> Prince Troilus, I have lov'd you night and day
> For many weary months.
> [III.ii.121–3]

When Troilus asks why she had seemed so hard to win, her reply is hesitant but frank:

> Hard to seem won; but I was won, my lord,
> With the first glance that ever—pardon me.
> If I confess much, you will play the tyrant.
> I love you now; but, till now, not so much
> But I might master it. In faith, I lie;
> My thoughts were like unbridled children, grown
> Too headstrong for their mother. See, we fools!
> Why have I blabb'd? Who shall be true to us,
> When we are so unsecret to ourselves?
> But, though I lov'd you well, I woo'd you not;
> And yet, good faith, I wish'd myself a man,
> Or that we women had men's privilege
> Of speaking first. Sweet, bid me hold my tongue,
> For in this rapture I shall surely speak
> The thing I shall repent. See, see, your silence,
> Cunning in dumbness, from my weakness draws
> My very soul of counsel. Stop my mouth.
>   [III.ii.125–41]

Of course, Cressida is faithless. That is according to the story, a story that the Middle Ages had invented and developed as part of the Trojan myth. But she is faithless with regret, and we must only with some reserve accept Ulysses' words on her after her arrival in the Greek camp:

>   Fie, fie upon her!
> There's language in her eye, her cheek, her lip,
> Nay, her foot speaks; her wanton spirits look out
> At every joint and motive of her body.
> O these encounterers so glib of tongue
> That give a coasting welcome ere it comes,
> And wide unclasp the tables of their thoughts
> To every ticklish reader! Set them down
> For sluttish spoils of opportunity,
> And daughters of the game.
>   [IV.v.54–63]

This is no more true than Ulysses' indiscriminate praise of Troilus in the same scene, where we are told: "Yet gives he not till judgment guide his bounty." We know that Troilus gave his heart to Cressida without judgment; we should recognize too that Cressida is not simply a "daughter of the game," a "sluttish spoil of opportunity." She is a woman who loved Troilus, but who could become faithless when he was far away and of no immediate succour to her. We may remember how Shakespeare in earlier plays showed his consciousness of the way a change of place can operate on behaviour. The dramatist is not concerned with denigrating Cressida here, but rather with showing the weaknesses to which human nature is generally incident.

Troilus, indeed, impresses us little more favourably than Cressida. She has a ready wit, and too ready a heart. He is devoted to her, but prepared at the same time to think she will be untrue to him. Even before their love is consummated, he is expressing doubts, declaring that he cannot be sure of any woman's faith. This is appropriate, for he had supported the continuation of a war for the possession of the faithless Helen, but it also brings the nature of his own love into question. That he himself will be faithful he is certain: no lover, he says, will be able to make a higher claim than that he is "As true as Troilus." Cressida protests in reply that, if she is false to him, she is ready for her name to become a byword for infidelity, for "As false as Cressid" to be the invariable description of faithless women. And her uncle Pandarus will not be left out: if there is any falseness at all between them, he is ready for all "brokers" in love to be called "Pandars." Here is rashness on all sides, but it has been provoked by Troilus' arrogant assertion of his own truth and his doubt of Cressida's.

When, on a visit to the Greek camp during a truce, Troilus finds that Cressida is false to him, he at first tries to convince himself that his eyes are deceiving him. If Cressida is false, he says to Ulysses, all women must be corrupt:

> Let it not be believ'd for womanhood.
> Think, we had mothers; do not give advantage
> To stubborn critics, apt, without a theme,
> For depravation, to square the general sex
> By Cressid's rule. Rather think this not Cressid.
> [V.ii.129-33]

Ulysses' reply is that of commonsense:

> What hath she done, Prince, that can soil our mothers?
> [V.ii.134]

Troilus has fallen into Hamlet's error, generalising from the stain on a particular woman to a belief in the frailty of all women. He tries not to believe, however, that there is identity between the woman he loved and coveted and, with a blind part of his mind, idealized, and the woman he now sees unfaithful. Of course, this mode of escape through unbelief will not work for long. His next way out is into revenge, and he swears vengeance on Cressida's new lover, Diomed. Shakespeare makes it plain enough in the concluding scenes of the play that Troilus' new-found enthusiasm for the war is a mode of re-directing his thwarted love-impulse.

This becomes overt at the very end. Troilus has spoken moving words of lamentation on the death of Hector, and once again has talked of revenge. But then Pandarus comes, plucking him by the sleeve, reminding him of their association in Cressida's love, in Cressida's loss. Troilus thrusts him away angrily, and resumes his mission to Troy with the terrible news of Hector's death. Pandarus remains behind to speak the play's epilogue, lamenting his own syphilitic condition, declaring his willingness to bequeathe

the disease to the spectators of the drama he has shared in. Troilus, still young, still active, can use war as a substitute for sexual strife. His go-between, whose help we saw him begging in the play's first scene, is old and decaying. But they have been engaged in the same affair. They have both enjoyed it in their different fashions. Now Pandarus is ready to fall apart, while Troilus will kill some more Greeks before he encounters his own death on the battle-field. As in the war story, the irony here is strong. Troilus before his union with Cressida could not persuade himself of her fidelity; when she has left him, he must kill men for her sake—as the Greeks and Trojans killed each other when Helen proved light.

In this play Shakespeare has used several choric, or semi-choric, characters. There is Pandarus, delighting in vicarious sexuality, looking beyond that only to sickness and dissolution, yet presiding over the wooing and coming together of the lovers who give the play its title. There is Thersites the Greek, who throughout expresses contempt for men on both sides in the war, seeing them all at the mercy of crude desire, the desire for military achievement, the desire for sexual assertion. "Lechery, lechery! Still wars and lechery! Nothing else holds fashion. A burning devil take them!" is his comment on the scene where Troilus learns of Cressida's infidelity and she exhibits her reluctant desertion of an absent lover in favour of the man ready at hand. And Ulysses is a kind of chorus too, expressing, as we have seen, admiration for Troilus and contempt for Cressida, speaking words of worldly wisdom to Achilles on the need to practise emulation, addressing the other Greek leaders on the need to suppress it. None of these figures can be taken as the dramatist's direct voice. They offer us half-truths, they are themselves the victims of their own characters, their own situations.

If we ask ourselves what Shakespeare leaves us with at the end of the play, I should say that two implications stand reasonably firm. First, he believes with Hector that value is not arbitrarily imposed: it is inherent in the thing itself, it is not in our power to give. That Hector fails to heed his own wisdom does not weaken the force of his assertion. Secondly, for all their imperfections, Shakespeare shows a measure of regard for human beings. We have noted how the frail Cressida expresses her love for the Troilus she will deceive. That it does not last does not mean this love is false. We should have an easier world if we could equate love and fidelity. And when they are to separate there is a real sense of grief in the lovers. Cressida may protest too violently, so that we recognize the shallowness of her grief's roots. But Troilus' words at their parting have a poignant authority as he sees their last moments together coming to an end, and savours the poor comfort of a kiss that knows it is the last:

> Injurious time now with a robber's haste
> Crams his rich thievery up, he knows not how.
> As many farewells as be stars in heaven,
> With distinct breath and consign'd kisses to them,
> He fumbles up into a loose adieu,
> And scants us with a single famish'd kiss,
> Distasted with the salt of broken tears.
> [IV.iii.44–50]

This is one of the play's many references to the power of Time. It will destroy all things—the love of two young people, the city of Troy, even the lives of Troy's conquerors. But *Troilus and Cressida*, for all its sharpness and frankness, is not a nihilistic play. There is a sense of pity here, a concern even for the apparently despicable. We cannot see this play without feeling in some measure that the sufferings and the frailties of the characters are our own. And we know too that their kind of joint enterprise, the waging of a war for a cause they do not fully believe in, the use of killing in the name of a tarnished love, is the kind of absurdity we see around us.

It is a harsh play, but also one of humanity and sympathy and appreciative laughter. All these qualities, together with its preoccupation with Time, appear again in *The Winter's Tale*, though there we find a wider range of dramatic mode and of characterization and incident and thought. The earlier play is more concentrated: despite its double action, with war and love thus brought together, *Troilus and Cressida* is one of the most disciplined of Shakespeare's plays. The play we shall now look at spans the generations and unites in an elaborate composition diverse ideas, diverse settings, diverse ways of conduct.

Its scene changes from Sicilia to Bohemia just before the end of Act III and then back to Sicilia for Act V. Moreover, sixteen years pass between Acts III and IV, time enough for Perdita to grow up and fall in love. We may be reminded of Sidney's description, in his *Apology for Poetry*, of the romantic plays of his own time, which he made fun of in this generalized comment:

ordinary it is that two young princes fall in love. After many traverses, she is got with child, delivered of a fair boy; he is lost, groweth a man, falls in love, and is ready to get another child; and all this in two hours' space: which, how absurd it is in sense, even sense may imagine, and Art hath taught, and all ancient examples justified, and, at this day, the ordinary players in Italy will not err in.[3]

Thus we find Shakespeare near the end of his career writing, it appears, the rambling kind of drama that antedated his beginnings, moving in a carefree fashion through a series of loosely linked incidents. Yet, if we observe *The Winter's Tale* closely, we shall I think find it anything but carefree.

First we may note that the play's act-division may mislead us. Act IV is one of the longest acts in Shakespearian drama, and the opening section in Sicilia, though extending over almost three acts, is only a little longer than the following section in Bohemia. These two sections of the play can thus be seen as balancing each other, and then there is a brief concluding section in which all the major Bohemians join the characters who have remained in Sicilia. And the fact that we move to Bohemia shortly before the sixteen-year time-lapse effects a bridge in space and time because the space- and time-leaps come at different moments.

Of the play's two worlds, Sicilia and Bohemia, that of Sicilia is quickly presented to us as a tormented and unideal place. We begin with a realistic prose conversation between Camillo, a Sicilian, and Archidamus, a Bohemian, and learn that Polixenes, King of Bohemia, has been visiting his boyhood friend Leontes, King of Sicilia. There is much formal compliment here, but the scene has a sharp ending:

ARCH. . . . You have an unspeakable comfort of your young Prince Mamillius; it is a gentleman of the greatest promise that ever came into my note.
CAM. I very well agree with you in the hopes of him. It is a gallant child; one that indeed physics the subject, makes old hearts fresh; they that went on crutches ere he was born desire yet their life to see him a man.
ARCH. Would they else be content to die?
CAM. Yes; if there were no other excuse why they should desire to live.
ARCH. If the King had no son, they would desire to live on crutches till he had one.

[I.i.37–50]

Then we meet Leontes and Polixenes, and see that Leontes is jealous of what he believes is his wife's love for Polixenes.

He has urged her to make Polixenes stay longer as a guest in Sicilia, but when she has prevailed he tortures himself with thoughts of her adultery:

> There have been,
> Or I am much deceiv'd, cuckolds ere now;
> And many a man there is, even at this present,
> Now while I speak this, holds his wife by th' arm
> That little thinks she has been sluic'd in's absence,
> And his pond fish'd by his next neighbour, by
> Sir Smile, his neighbour. Nay, there's comfort in't,
> Whiles other men have gates and those gates open'd,
> As mine, against their will. Should all despair
> That have revolted wives, the tenth of mankind
> Would hang themselves. Physic for't there's none;
> It is a bawdy planet, that will strike
> When 'tis predominant; and 'tis pow'rful, think it,
> From east, west, north, and south. Be it concluded,
> No barricado for a belly. Know't,
> It will let in and out the enemy
> With bag and baggage. Many thousand on's
> Have the disease, and feel't not.
> [I.ii.190–207]

Nowhere else in Shakespeare is there so frank and tormenting a picture of a husband's jealousy: Othello never used imagery as gross as this. Here indeed the images of disgust tumble out in the most painful kind of tangential association. There may well be a hint in it all that Leontes is more jealous of Polixenes than of his wife Hermione, that it is the loss of a boyhood friend that is the unacknowledged root of his anguish. Certainly Polixenes' elaborate description earlier in the scene of his shared boyhood with Leontes, and the indication of their joint sense of loss when they grew up, separated, and married, give support to this. In both men there is a feeling of guilt in their relations with women. Above all, however, we are made aware that Leontes needs no Iago to prompt him to jealousy: he is simply a man who has fallen ill in the dangerous world that he and we inhabit.

Yet in that world dignity is possible, though Leontes in this part of the play does not achieve it. Hermione can speak with reticent authority when, shortly after being delivered of her daughter Perdita, she is brought to stand trial on a capital charge. Like Queen Katharine in the later play *Henry VIII*, she appeals to outside authority, mentioning the Emperor of Russia as her father and the oracle of Apollo as her sole acceptable judge:

> Sir, spare your threats.
> The bug which you would fright me with I seek.
> To me can life be no commodity.
> The crown and comfort of my life, your favour,
> I do give lost, for I do feel it gone,
> But know not how it went; my second joy
> And first fruits of my body, from his presence
> I am barr'd, like one infectious; my third comfort,
> Starr'd most unluckily, is from my breast—
> The innocent milk in it most innocent mouth—
> Hal'd out to murder; myself on every post
> Proclaim'd a strumpet; with immodest hatred
> The child-bed privilege denied, which 'longs
> To women of all fashion; lastly, hurried
> Here to this place, i' th' open air, before
> I have got strength of limit. Now, my liege,
> Tell me what blessings I have here alive
> That I should fear to die. Therefore proceed.
> But yet hear this—mistake me not: no life,
> I prize it not a straw, but for mine honour
> Which I would free—if I shall be condemn'd
> Upon surmises, all proofs sleeping else
> But what your jealousies awake, I tell you
> 'Tis rigour, and not law. Your honours all,
> I do refer me to the oracle:
> Apollo be my judge!
>
> 1 LORD.   This your request

Is altogether just. Therefore, bring forth,
And in Apollo's name, his oracle. . . .
HER. The Emperor of Russia was my father;
O that he were alive, and here beholding
His daughter's trial! that he did but see
The flatness of my misery; yet with eyes
Of pity, not revenge!

[III.ii.92–124]

Leontes' authority shrinks here, as we are reminded that there are other sovereign princes and that a divine voice may be consulted.

The oracle is important in the play. In *Pericles* Diana had appeared in person to the hero and urged him to go to Ephesus, where he would find his lost wife Thaisa. In *Cymbeline* Jupiter came in majesty to Posthumus Leonatus when he was in prison and awaiting death, and left with him a riddling message of hope. But in *The Winter's Tale* there is no direct manifestation of the god. Shakespeare had doubtless come to realize that, even in the world of romance, gods can function with greater authority if the mode of their presentation is indirect. So at the opening of the third act we meet Cleomenes and Dion, the two messengers who have been sent to Apollo's oracle from Sicilia, and they exchange words on the solemnities they have witnessed and their hope for the Queen. The contrast of the ceremonial at the shrine with the feverish activities of Leontes' court makes this scene, so frequently cut in performance, of high importance in the play:

CLEO. The climate's delicate, the air most sweet,
Fertile the isle, the temple much surpassing
The common praise it bears.
DIO.   I shall report,
For most it caught me, the celestial habits—
Methinks I so should term them—and the reverence
Of the grave wearers. O, the sacrifice!

How ceremonious, solemn, and unearthly,
It was i' th' off'ring!
CLEO.   But of all, the burst
And the ear-deaf'ning voice o' th' oracle,
Kin to Jove's thunder, so surpris'd my sense
That I was nothing.
DIO.   If th' event o' th' journey
Prove as successful to the Queen—O, be't so!—
As it hath been to us rare, pleasant, speedy,
The time is worth the use on't.
CLEO.   Great Apollo
Turn all to th' best! These proclamations,
So forcing faults upon Hermione,
I little like.
DIO.   The violent carriage of it
Will clear or end the business. When the oracle—
Thus by Apollo's great divine seal'd up—
Shall the contents discover, something rare
Even then will rush to knowledge. Go; fresh horses.
And gracious be the issue!

                                      [III.i.1–22]

Yet, in further counterpoint to all this, we have throughout the play a series of references to an "old" or "winter's"
tale and to the action as a theatrical one, which repeatedly
remind us that we are watching a play and a presentation
of a fabulous story. This is not life as we know it, we are
again and again assured, though it may have the authority
that comes from ancient tale-telling or current ceremonial.
It is an emblem, not a replica. Thus the very title of the
play we are seeing is echoed as Hermione talks with her
son Mamillius just before she is unexpectedly removed to
prison:

HER. . . .   Pray you sit by us,
And tell's a tale.
MAM.   Merry or sad shall't be?
HER. As merry as you will.
MAM. A sad tale's best for winter. I have one
Of sprites and goblins.

HER.   Let's have that, good sir.
    Come on, sit down; come on, and do your best
    To fright me with your sprites; you're pow'rful at it.
MAM. There was a man—
HER.   Nay, come, sit down; then on.
MAM. Dwelt by a churchyard—I will tell it softly;
    Yond crickets shall not hear it.
HER.   Come on then,
    And give't me in mine ear.
                                        [II.i.22–32]

When she is brought to her trial, Hermione insists that her
innocent anguish exceeds anything that a history play has
presented on the stage:

                You, my lord, best know—
        Who least will seem to do so—my past life
        Hath been as continent, as chaste, as true,
        As I am now unhappy; which is more
        Than history can pattern, though devis'd
        And play'd to take spectators.
                                        [III.ii.33–8]

When Time appears as the chorus to bridge the gap
between Acts III and IV, he refers to the action of the play
as "my tale," and in the following act Camillo talks to the
Prince Florizel of "the scene you play." So Perdita can
remark: "I see the play so lies / That I must bear a part."
When we come to Act V, Leontes' recognition of Perdita
as his daughter is more than once described as being like
something from "an old tale," and one of the Gentlemen
who give a report on the meeting presents it in terms of a
theatrical show:

The dignity of this act was worth the audience of kings and
princes; for by such was it acted. [V.ii.86–8]

So, when the apparent statue of Hermione turns out to be
the living woman, who has remained in hiding for sixteen
years, her attendant Paulina says that a simple statement
of the truth would be "hooted like an old tale," and the

very last words of the play contain a theatrical image, when
Leontes says:

> Good Paulina,
> Lead us from hence where we may leisurely
> Each one demand and answer to his part
> Perform'd in this wide gap of time since first
> We were dissever'd. Hastily lead away.
>
> [V.iii.151–5]

Thus we are bidden to remember that the action as presented is a fantastic one, to be associated with ancient
romance and the extravagances of the theatre. But that, as
we shall see, has a special significance in this play.

For one thing, because we have been reminded that we
are being shown the events of a world of the fancy, we can
accommodate ourselves to the Bohemian pastoral setting so
prominent in the second half of the play. But this country
of Bohemia is not entirely different from the Sicilia we
have seen hitherto. Though there is order and a plain
dignity in the shepherds' festival, life in this place can have
its melodramatic denunciations as well as its romantic love,
its hints of shabbiness as well as its lyrical fluency. One of
the most remarkable passages here is that between Perdita
and Polixenes on the subject of Nature and Art, which is
prompted by Perdita's giving to Polixenes and Camillo
flowers that "keep / Seeming and savour all the winter
long":

Pol.   Shepherdess—
    A fair one are you—well you fit our ages
    With flow'rs of winter.
Per.   Sir, the year growing ancient.
    Not yet on summer's death nor on the birth
    Of trembling winter, the fairest flow'rs o' th' season
    Are our carnations and streak'd gillyvors,
    Which some call nature's bastards. Of that kind
    Our rustic garden's barren; and I care not
    To get slips of them.

POL.	Wherefore, gentle maiden,
	Do you neglect them?
PER.	For I have heard it said
	There is an art which in their piedness shares
	With great creating nature.
POL.	Say there be;
	Yet nature is made better by no mean
	But nature makes that mean; so over that art,
	Which you say adds to nature, is an art
	That nature makes. You see, sweet maid, we marry
	A gentler scion to the wildest stock,
	And make conceive a bark of baser kind
	By bud of nobler race. This is an art
	Which does mend nature—change it rather; but
	The art itself is nature.
PER.	So it is.
POL.	Then make your garden rich in gillyvors,
	And do not call them bastards.
PER.	I'll not put
	The dibble in earth to set one slip of them;
	No more than were I painted I would wish
	This youth should say 'twere well, and only therefore
	Desire to breed by me.

[IV.iv.77–103]

Perdita is intellectually persuaded but obstinate; Polixenes does not apply his doctrine to his own family, refusing to let the "bark of baser kind" (Perdita as he thinks of her) "conceive / By bud of nobler race" (Florizel in this instance); and on both of them a jest is being played, for Perdita too fails to see the relevance of Polixenes' doctrine to her own apparent situation, and Polixenes is mistaken in thinking Perdita a girl of humble stock. The play implies a need for the application of Art—man's fashioning of Nature to his purpose—to the general conduct of life. Throughout the action Leontes and Polixenes have acted with too much spontaneity, responding immediately to the impulse provided by a momentary situation. Later Hermione has first to appear as the alleged creation of an artist

—the sculptor Giulio Romano—before things can be brought into order. The Art, moreover, that man uses is part of the natural order that man himself belongs to: human nature and its capacities are included within "great creating nature"; to make is to contribute to the stream of creation, while at the same time it is to resist the mere flowing of the stream. It is a characteristic complexity of this play that one of its key notions is introduced in what appears at first to be a merely romantic and comparatively carefree pastoral world. In passing I have referred to a certain shabbiness in that world. There are several signs of it, but most notably perhaps it appears in the behaviour of Camillo when he persuades Florizel and Perdita to make their way to Sicilia and then betrays them to Polixenes, simply because he is homesick and thinks this is an opportunity for him to see Sicilia again when Polixenes is pursuing his son. At this stage, of course, Camillo has no idea that Perdita is Leontes' daughter.

Art is needed, but not this kind of artfulness. Art is needed in particular because Time brings decay. This is not a play without death: the young prince Mamillius dies so that Leontes shall realize his crime of blasphemy when he refuses to credit Apollo's statement of Hermione's innocence; Antigonus is devoured by a bear when he has left Perdita on the Bohemian shore; a whole shipload of men perish in the storm that follows. The destructiveness of Nature, in fact, is not passed silently by. Those that are left either grow up or grow old. When Leontes sees what he thinks is his wife's statue, he is astonished that it presents her as so much older than he remembers her:

> But yet, Paulina,
> Hermione was not so much wrinkled, nothing
> So aged as this seems.
>
> [V.iii.27–9]

But of course it is Hermione herself who has acquired the

wrinkles. We may think back to Shakespeare's sonnets and recall that there Art is seen as the sole survivor of an otherwise universal destruction wrought by Time. For indeed, however powerful the repentance for the lost years, Time cannot be regained, and the natural life is mere disorder. But here the significance of Art has become broader than in the sonnets: it includes the controlling of our own conduct of life, the manipulation of natural experience, our own and that of others, in accordance with a notion of what is fitting. By man's application of Art to Nature, something coherent can be made.

So the continual references to "an old tale" and to the theatre have a special relevance in *The Winter's Tale*. This play itself is a thing made, a contrived image of human life. That is what we have to concern ourselves with as we go through the experience of living, the making of the flux into something coherent, something achieved, something humanly controlled. We are not promised success, but the attempt is demanded of us.[4]

In these two comedies with which I have concluded my comments on one section of Shakespeare's work, we have had, I believe, major works under scrutiny. They go beyond "delight," they offer us, rather, a sharp analysis of folly, a reminder in both plays of the operations of Time, and in *The Winter's Tale* an insistence that only by a making of artifacts can we achieve some control over the flux of things.

> The boat responded
> Gaily, to the hand expert with sail and oar
> The sea was calm, your heart would have responded
> Gaily, when invited, beating obedient
> To controlling hands—

Eliot's words in *The Waste Land* could retrospectively function as an epigraph to *The Winter's Tale*, and in *Troilus and Cressida* we see Time's destructiveness without remission. It was, I think, to a larger vision of comedy that Shakespeare reached when he passed beyond the vulnerable "delight" of *Twelfth Night, or What You Will.* And as he faced the ruins of Time, the destructiveness of impulse, his mastery grew assured. There is no sense that what is being done in these plays could easily fall apart. With "delight" no longer a primary concern, the artifact is firmly made.

NOTES TO LECTURE III

1. *Troilus* was originally to have been printed in the "Tragedies" section after *Romeo and Juliet*. For some reason
   the printing was interrupted, and the play (still headed
   "The Tragedie of Troylus and Cressida") finally
   appeared between the "Histories" and the "Tragedies."
2. In *Shakespeare's Tragedies and Other Studies in Seventeenth Century Drama* (London, 1950), p. 31, I have
   suggested that the very fullness of Ulysses' formulation
   of the idea implies that the matter, no longer to be
   taken for granted, is presented in this play for unpreju-
   diced scrutiny.
3. *English Critical Essays (Sixteenth, Seventeenth, and
   Eighteenth Centuries)*, ed. Edmund D. Jones (World's
   Classics, 1922), p. 54.
4. It is a characteristic of the so-called last plays (a label that
   disregards the later collaboration with Fletcher) that
   there is no promise of immunity for the next generation,
   whose saluting of a "brave new world" (*The Tempest*,
   V.i.183) is seen ironically by at least one of the older
   people. I have commented further on this in "The
   Structure of the Last Plays," *Shakespeare Survey* 11
   (1958), pp. 19–30.

Milton Keynes UK
Ingram Content Group UK Ltd.
UKHW031030291024
450383UK00004B/124

9 781487 577117